DAIWA

GW01071935

Welcome

Welcome to The Complete Coarse Fisherman, a resource designed to help you gain a better understanding about the UK's favourite fish species and how to catch them.

The freshwaters around the UK offer myriad exciting, beautiful and challenging fish species. Here we cover everything from roach and perch to commercial carp and pike, bringing you the best advice and guidance from some of the country's top anglers, specifically aimed at helping you get more from your fishing.

Produced by the team behind the brilliant monthly angling magazine Total Coarse Fishing, you can expect the same level of expertise and knowledge, along with stunning photography and easy-to-understand tips, tactics and advice.

All that's left to do now is dive in, enjoy yourself and get out there on the bank to put everything you learn into action for yourself.

Tight lines.

Steve Phillips
Editor, Total Coarse Fishing

Contents

Compiled and edited by **Steve Phillips**
Layout and design by **Fiona Brett**
Sub edited by **David Haynes** and **Rob Bradley**
Reprographics by **Derek Mooney** and **Adam Mason**

Roach
Rutilus rutilus

The 'bread and butter' fish of the British angler, the roach is loved by all. The joy of matchmen, a coveted prize of the speci set and a firm favourite of the pleasure angler, they are present and fished for right across the full range of UK waters, from canals and rivers to commercials and lochs.

The species' abundance and hardiness has seen it almost become taken for granted by angling, and whether it's 1oz or 4lb they are always a welcome sight on the hook. But it's the range of challenges that the fish offers where their real appeal lies.

Not the easiest of fish to catch, but not so hard that they test anglers to their limits, they present the novice with an achievable target, while also giving the more accomplished angler a good work out to catch in good numbers. On the specimen front the bigger a roach gets the wiser it becomes, making anything over 1½lb a quarry you need to put the effort in to catch.

As a weight target it's the 2lb barrier that's the goal. For most a roach of this size is a fish of a lifetime, and one that it can take decades to achieve. Reach 3lb and it's a capture that you can dine out on for the rest of your life, while a four is the stuff of legend and worthy of historic recognition.

Another aspect of the roach's popularity is that they can be caught on a multitude of baits. Although bread, hemp and casters are the more traditional roach catchers, they will take anything from plastic sweetcorn and worms to boilies and elderberries. Add this to the list of tactics that they can be caught on and you are looking at the ultimate everyman fish.

The Facts

Record: 4lb 4oz caught by Keith Berry from a Northern Irish stillwater, 2006
Max weight: 5lb
Max length: 18 inches
Max age: 15 years
Specimen weight: 2lb
Spawn: Between April and May depending on temperatures

Venues

Lochnaw Castle Loch, Galloway, southwest Scotland
Fast becoming a Mecca for big roach, the water in the castle grounds has produced a string of 3lb fish over the past year.

Dorset Stour, Dorset
The roach angler's river, the Stour has produced a number of a big fish over the years, including possibly the most famous of the species' record fish in 1990 of 4lb 3oz. There's not so many fish now, but if you hook one, it's going to be good.

Willow Pool, Linch Hill, Oxfordshire
Running a small, winter roach syndicate, Linch Hill's Willow Pool has produced fish to 4lb in the past, with a number of threes and plenty of twos to target.

Roach Rewards

Preston Innovations-backed match ace Lee Kerry unlocks the tactics for finding, feeding and catching canal roach – and you can do it too!

Fact File
Name: Lee Kerry
Age: 30
Sponsors: Preston Innovations

I f I could catch just one species for the rest of my life it would have to be roach. In my angling career I've probably caught double the amount of roach than I have any other species, but I can assure you that when my alarm went off this morning for this feature I still couldn't wait to get on the bank to catch a load more.

Today I have come to the Stainforth & Keadby Canal to see if I can catch some quality redfins for the TCF cameras. I know this length of canal has got a lot of roach in it, but the better specimens definitely have their preferred winter hotspots, which goes to highlight that the key to success with these fish at any time of the year, but especially in winter, is location. First find the fish, then figure out the best way of catching them.

So what do you look for when trying to locate big roach? Being a match angler at heart the first thing I do is check out my local angling news. There's a nonstop stream of information available these days, so look out for the match results; these often have peg numbers listed in them, which is a great starting place. Once I've identified likely venues, it is then time to apply some watercraft to identify the best spots.

Location, Location, Location

In winter the first thing to consider is an element of cover. Roach, by nature, are nervous creatures, they swim around in large shoals for protection so any form of safety will be a likely holding spot. My swim today is a perfect example.

Along this relatively uniform canal, there is suddenly a change where the canal widens to nearly three times its normal width. This ▶

Big, loaded wagglers give less splash on entry, more stability in the wind and sensitive bite indication.

A lovely brace of big canal roach. Follow Lee's advice and this could be you.

opening is a marina, and a lot of boats have moored up for winter here. With many of those boats containing permanent residents, the water underneath will be warmer and will limit the amount of daylight on the water, giving the fish a sense of safety. Any one of these features would be a natural holding spot for fish, but put them all together and you have a winter hotspot that is likely to hold not only plenty of fish but, importantly for the roach enthusiast, also the big 'uns!

As the water gets warmer I'd consider other features such as overhanging trees, turning bays or where the locals go to feed the ducks! Crucially, though, it's the warmer water that will encourage the fish to congregate in winter so, if you are looking at your local venue, consider these aspects carefully before deciding where to sit.

Weighty Issues

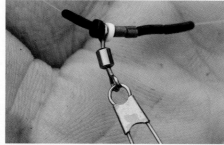

Lee uses a loaded wag held in place by float stops and Stotz, creating a boom effect to reduce tangles.

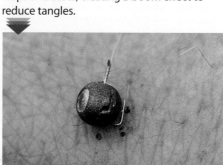

By shotting the float correctly and then adding a No1 shot to the hook plumbing up is accurate and doesn't scare the fish.

Tackle Approach

Once you've chosen your swim the next consideration is how to tackle it. There are many methods popular for big roach, but on a large, natural venue such as this I don't want to be too selective as there are many other species around such as skimmers, perch and bream. With this in mind I've chosen to base today's approach around casters and maggots. These really are baits that will catch everything, and casters in particular always seem to attract the better quality fish in the swim.

They also work well with today's chosen method, the waggler. Waggler fishing is one of my favourite forms of angling, because there's real skill required to present your float in the correct place, and achieve the best presentation.

The reason I've gone for a waggler today is because in front of me is the opening to the marina. The canal widens to over 30 metres and either side of the marina is flanked with boats. The opening is bound to attract fish, but at over 16 metres away it's out of pole range, and if I'm loose feeding casters, the fish will prefer the presentation to come from a slow-falling bait, which rules out the feeder. Of course, the weather conditions may mean a waggler isn't always suitable, but on days with little wind, or the wind at your back, then it's a great choice.

Plumb It

Plumbing up correctly on a waggler is something that took me a while to get right. One of the reasons it's a problem is that if you attach a plummet, the weight of the float at one end and the plummet at the other causes the rig to spin on the cast, and often come crashing down into the water – not ideal for wary fish. So instead I set up my waggler rig so it's correctly shotted, with only a centimetre of the tip showing, then I attach a No1 shot directly to the hook. By doing this I can smoothly cast out into the peg and adjust the depth little by little to ensure I know exactly where the bottom is. I always then mark it on my rod to ensure I know that depth at all times. My starting depth is nearly always 15cm overdepth to be sure my bait's laying stationary on the bottom, and I won't be afraid to have up to two feet on or off the bottom if conditions require.

Kit Choice

The setup on the wag is very straightforward; however, it's important to get things right, otherwise problems can occur that can severely hamper your day's fishing.

Today I have a 13ft float rod – this length offers me good line pickup and is easy to handle, the rod has to be quite forgiving because relatively light hooks and line will be used, so anything too stiff will result in poor casting and lost fish.

For my reel line I am using 0.13mm Reflo Power; this is a hi-tech line not usually associated with fishing as a main line on a reel, but I can assure you it is perfect for the job. It's very supple but has a high breaking strain, meaning it can take plenty of casting abuse. More importantly, the thin diameter offers very little resistance to the float when casting. This in turn allows a lighter float to be used, which means less resistance to finicky roach.

When using a light line I try to avoid using big shot, so the float for the session is a preloaded Preston Insert Dura Wag locked in place using sliding float stops. These not only hold the float in place, but also create a boom effect at the bottom of the float, pushing the line away from the tip and drastically reducing tangles. I'll often put Preston Stotz here as well; ▸

Shoal Thinking

In winter you're looking for the areas on the canal where the roach will be shoaling. The boats of a marina mean cover from predators, extra warmth (it doesn't take much to make a spot a des res for roach) and food. All of which mean that the roach should be there, and in numbers too.

Distance

Lee found his fish across the main body of the canal into the marina area around the boats. This meant the pole was ruled out due to the distance, making the waggler the ultimate approach for plundering the roach shoals that were in residence.

these won't damage the line and will ensure the float is shotted correctly.

Further down the rig are four No9 shot at 20cm intervals, with a small No14 match swivel above a 30cm hooklength. The swivel is a must as the very nature of waggler fishing means you'll be winding in and out a lot, so without a swivel the hooklength will simply spin up and need replacing very quickly. To assist this I also try and fish as heavy a hooklength as possible, and with the odd bonus fish expected today I have a 0.09mm hooklength to an 18 PR 344 hook. This can be stepped down to a 0.08mm and PR 333 if the fishing's difficult, but always start with the strongest hooklength you can.

Feed 'Em

Loose-fed casters are my chosen feed and to kick off I fire two large pouchfuls across the bay. They, of course, spread all over, but when you're fishing a waggler in conjunction with loose feed, the idea is to create competition between the fish, and make them actively move around the peg looking for food. As you fish you can gauge the response of the fish and adjust the feeding to suit. For example, after the initial burst I start to feed around 20 casters every cast and quickly have two 4oz roach, followed by a series of small perch – a sign that there are a lot of feeding fish in the peg, so I up the feed to a near full pouch after every fish.

This works well and I have a run of roach including a cracking fish around 1lb. Everything's going smoothly, then a quiet spell occurs, which could mean a pike's moved in.

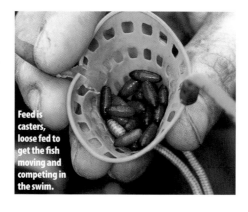

Feed is casters, loose fed to get the fish moving and competing in the swim.

A 13ft rod gives Lee the power to cast the float out and strike into fish.

Some people may be tempted to stop feeding at this time, not wanting to fill the peg with feed if there are no fish there. This is unlikely to ever see the fish return, though, so I tend to reduce the feed down to the original 20 or so casters. This works, with the roach soon returning, so I again increase the feed to create competition.

The Results

Towards the end of the session, other fish put in an appearance. A series of hybrids, followed by a bream of around 3lb, finish off what can only be described as a fantastic day's fishing.

Even though the weather's cold, today's session has proved that the rewards are there to be had in winter – pick the right time, place and method and catches to remember really are possible. ∎

What a haul! It shows just what's possible with the right location and techniques.

Top Roach Hooks

• **Kamasan B511**
A classic light-line, small-fish hook, perfect for targeting roach on the pole with great presentation.

• **Drennan Fine Match**
Super lightweight to aid presentation, this pattern is also highly durable.

• **Tubertini Series 2 Bronze**
A favourite pattern for many a roach bagger, it offers a round-bend pattern in a medium-thickness wire.

• **Preston Innovations PR 333**
A great hook for targeting smaller fish on natural venues, made from carbon steel.

INTELLIGENT
TACKLE

Redesigned to help transform your fishing.
A bag to suit every angler.

MANAGEMENT

RUCKSACK

Floating D Ring and caribeners for attaching spoon nets • Insulated top bait compartment • Webbing loops for unhooking mats or waterproofs • Front harness for clothing • Front load access • Ergonomic harness with chest and waist belt • Reinforced zipped base compartment • Tackle box compatible front pocket • External side pockets • Dirt resistant EVA base • FREE Korum Rig Manager • 33cm wide x 20cm deep x 56cm high

ROVING RUCKSACK

Floating D Ring and caribeners for attaching spoon nets • Insulated top bait compartment • Webbing loops for unhooking mats or waterproofs • Ergonomic harness with chest strap • Mesh zip pocket on the front pocket • Reinforced zipped base compartment • 50cm wide x 30cm deep x 36cm high

DAY SACK

Built in chest strap • Floating D Ring and caribeners for attaching spoon nets • Webbing loops for unhooking mats • Two external mesh pockets • Fully padded harness system • Dirt resistant EVA base • ITM compatible front pocket • Straps to take the unhooking mats or waterproofs • 34cm wide x 20cm deep x 38cm high

Fishing Made Easy

www.korum.co.uk

In Search Of Giants

Editor Steve Phillips heads north of the border to a land where giants roam free and anglers cast with bated breath.

Fact File

Name: Gareth Goldson
Occupation: Tennis coach
Roach PB: 3lb 2oz – two from Lochnaw Castle Loch, Scotland

It's amazing how a bit of fishing can get you out of bed when nothing else will. Most of the time it'd take dynamite to get me out of my pit, but dangle the carrot of a bit of angling in and I'll be up without a murmur of a yawn.

The carrot on this occasion was a big and juicy example… a couple of days fishing at one of the UK's best big-roach waters. Not only that, but I'd be alongside Drennan Cup champion Gareth Goldson – it was an angling adventure extraordinaire. I was there with bells on.

The adventure began early. Leaving the Midlands at an ungodly time I was on the M6 through Birmingham, past Manchester and across the Scottish border in four hours. A left turn saw the writhing A75 lead all the way to Stranraer. Ten minutes further on, after a total of six hours' driving, there was the destination – the famous Lochnaw Castle loch.

The home of gentle giants, the loch is a beautiful sight. Enclosed by woods, fringed by lilies and overseen by the venue's 600-year-old castle, it's steeped in history… but it's not what's visible above the waterline that's of interest.

Since coarse fishing was allowed on the 50-acre water last year, Lochnaw has exploded onto the big-fish scene with captures of specimen roach that anglers can normally only dream of. Thanks to its shallow topography, an abundance of natural food and lack of predators, its resident roach have grown huge. Three-pound fish are common, twos 10 a penny – catch one below the magic two and you're unlucky. What a place!

The loch doesn't give up its residents easily, though, you have to work for your catch. But get it right and the rewards will blow your mind. And if any man could get it right on this trip it would be recently crown Drennan Cup Champion Gareth Goldson.

Last year Lochnaw produced one of the fish that helped win him his title, and this year he's back for more, and hopefully bigger.

Gareth has already been bankside on the loch for three days when I find him in a far corner of the water. Fishing's been slow, but he did have an upper 2lb fish on his first day and he's confidence something special could happen.

"You never know with this place," smiles Gareth as we stick the kettle on. "Last week all the guys here caught, but only in small numbers, while the week before they were having huge catches of big fish."

Brew gulped, shelter up and rods assembled it's time to find out what tactics are working.

"I like to keep it simple and I'm a big fan of

a groundbait approach for big roach, especially here where there could be a number of fish to keep occupied," explains Gareth. For this he uses a mix of Dynamite Baits Silver X Roach Super Black and Dynamite Baits Frenzied Hemp, adding a small number of 10mm The Source boilies and a dose of ylang ylang essential oil.

Feeding is regimented. After using a Nash Deliverance 40mm ball maker Gareth fires out 15 balls via catapult. "I'm fishing at about 50 yards range," explains Gareth, "but because the loch is so shallow I can wade out around 20 yards, making my feeding much more accurate."

Although he could feed a tight area, he opts to spread them over a patch of around four metres square, giving the big roach a good-sized spot to find and get their head down over.

This barrage of bait happens early morning and late evening, and with this instalment in place it's time to get his rigs out. "I'm using a helicopter setup with a cage feeder," Gareth tells me. "I'm using a cage feeder because the water's shallow, so I know the groundbait will get down to the bottom but break down." ▶

Up from the feeder, tied directly to the 8lb main line via a link swivel, is a short hook link of 6lb line rotating around the main line on a swivel held between two float stops. This carries a size 16 hook with a single 10mm The Source boilie hair rigged off its back.

"I use boilies here as it cuts out the smaller fish picking up the bait. The Source boilies are good for pretty much any species I've come across," reveals Gareth.

Again he wades out to cast. Two rods are fished at opposite edges of the feed area, with the third dropped just out of the baited zone.

"I've had a number of bigger fish by doing this," says Gareth. "The smaller fish dive into the bait, the large, more canny fish will hold off around the fringes, but if they happen to find a small pile of bait and a single boilie away from the crowd they can't help but feed."

With the rods cast out and on the alarms it's now a waiting game. Gareth will only move his rods if a fish takes, or on the following morning or evening. "I don't like to move my bait – once it's in it's in," he smiles.

As the sun sinks away, expectations are high. "I've found they normally feed between 11pm and 1am," he explains. But after retiring to the shelter of our respective brollies we have an undisturbed sleep. That is until around 4am the following

Into darkness Gareth waits for a take from what could be a Scottish giant.

What we came for – a brace of big roach both over the magical 3lb mark.

morning. In complete contrast to the sunshine and warmth of the previous day a cold wind is tearing across the loch, driving rain with it.

"It's horrible for us, but it's perfect for the roach to get feeding," says Gareth. "The wind kicks up the shallow water of the loch, with all sorts of undertows spreading out the scent from the swim and helping draw fish in. The chop on the surface and the overcast sky are exactly how I want it."

Almost as if the roach have heard him, not long after being recast the middle of his three rods registers a bite. The alarms delivers a trio of bleeps as the bobbin rises slowly and stays there, giving Gareth time to get in his waders and lift into the bite.

"It's a good fish," he utters as his Hardy Marksman Supero Avon rod hoops over. With the water so shallow close in, Gareth wades out to a decent netting depth. A few heart-stopping minutes later and he's heading back in, net sagging, big smile – "It's a three!"

The scales seal the deal, with the needle spinning round to deliver the verdict of 3lb and half an ounce.

Now, like the majority of anglers, I have never seen a 3lb roach in the flesh before. The depth of this fish was staggering, the pure mass of it jaw dropping; I was like a schoolboy in my excitement – but there was even better to come. Thanks to the continued driving rain, the roach is gently placed in Gareth's keepnet until a lull in the weather for photos and who knew, we joke, we might be able to get a brace of threes…

Again, on cue, the roach hear and obey. This time the third rod placed off the bait delivers a duo of bleeps before the bobbin rises. Out in the water the lack of commentary and the look of concentration on his face signal that Gareth knows this is an even bigger fish.

It hits the back of the net to a cry of laughter from the both of us. Straight to the scales and Gareth's thoughts are confirmed, and we're both looking at a stunning specimen roach of 3lb 2oz – the third at this weight that Gareth's caught from two venues and one that equals his personal best yet again.

A lull in the weather and we have both fish on the unhooking mat in front of the camera. That's two roach for over 6lb we're staring at. It's an unbelievable sight and one I suspect I'll never witness again. As angling adventures go this has been a truly amazing 24 hours on the bank and, although the effort's needed to make it happen, the experience is one I'd recommend to every red-blooded angler out there. ∎

Rudd
Scardinius erythrophthalmus

The Facts
Record: 4lb 10oz caught from a lake in Co Armargh, Northern Ireland in 2001
Max weight: 5lb
Max length: 18 inches
Max age: 15 years
Specimen weight: 2lb
Spawn: May to early June

Like sunshine in fish form, the golden-flanked rudd is synonymous with the long, hazy days of summer. Easily one of the prettiest fish in our waters, in smaller sizes the rudd is a voracious feeder and can be caught in large numbers, usually in the top half of the water using pole and waggler tactics.

A classic resident of farm ponds and shallow estate lakes, rudd can range in colour from the stereotypical yellow-gold hue, through oranges and light browns depending on the environment they're swimming in. Wherever they are present, though, they add excitement and colour to an angling session.

At the upper end of their size scale they become a much cannier quarry, requiring patience to feed them into a false sense of security. Anatomically the species' underslung mouth makes it perfectly adapted for feeding up in the water, sipping insects and other food flotsam delicately from the surface film – get them going right up in the water and, for angling thrills, targeting them right on the surface takes some beating.

Similar to roach in looks, the differentiating features, other than that of the underslung mouth, are that the dorsal fin is further back along the body and that the number of scales between the tip of the pelvic fin and the anal fin on the rudd is much fewer than found on roach.

Whatever the size, wherever they're caught and however you catch them, though, bring a rudd to the bank and we dare you not to smile at one of the most aesthetically pleasing and fun fish you're likely to catch.

Venues

River Cam, Cambridgeshire
The Waterbeach Angling Club stretch of this slow-flowing river holds a good head of large rudd.

Horseshoe Lake, Gloucestershire
Run by the Carp Society, as well as large carp Horseshoe also holds plenty of specimen rudd – and they're accessible on a day ticket.

Frensham Great Pond, Surrey
There are some whacking great rudd in this shallow lake run by Farnham Angling Society.

King's Sedgemoor Drain, Somerset
For small rudd fishing the Somerset levels are hard to beat, with the Sedgemoor a great start.

Get On The Blob

When it comes to fast-paced, close-range, shallow fishing there are few tactics as effective as the basic blob, as Korum's Chris Ponsford demonstrates.

Fact File
Name: Chris Ponsford
Age: 60
Occupation: Works for the EA

There are many people that would argue that over recent years the art of fishing has become a little overcomplicated. Massively detailed shotting patterns with exotic floats for every angling situation, hair-rigged everything and setups that require a PhD in lateral thinking to both construct and cast, let alone keep from tangling.

But that doesn't always need to be the case. Although detailed setups will undoubtedly catch you fish, you can also have plenty of fun on one of the most basic and easiest to fish approaches you're ever likely to see – and here we introduce the blob.

"This is as simple as it gets, but it's deadly effective, even more so than standard float setups on its day," Korum's all-rounder ace Chris Ponsford tells TCF as he makes his first cast of the day. We say cast, but it's more of a whip action, with Chris totally ignoring the reel and fishing his Korum 11ft CS Series rod as if it were, in fact, a whip.

"You could fish the blob on the whip and it would effectively be the same approach," explains Chris, "but when I'm fishing a venue like this with a few carp about I like to have the backup of a reel just in case I need to give line. An 11ft rod is perfect for the job as you can fish easily to hand and still get a good distance out."

But what is the blob exactly? Well the name says it all. A buoyant, spherical, surface bite indicator, the blob attaches to your line like a float stop, with the main line sitting through the centre of the 'float'.

"It grips the line but can be easily moved up and down to change the depth that your hook bait is fished at," says Chris. "The key thing is that it doesn't intrude into the swim as it just sits on the surface, making it perfect for fishing really shallow, targeting species like rudd and roach when they're up in the water."

And that's exactly what we're after today. Visiting Astwood Fishery in Worcestershire we're targeting the venue's big shoals of quality rudd on Smokie Joe's lake – and they're suckers for a well-fished blob.

Chris is looking to catch his quarry just a rod length out. "Why make it more difficult for yourself?" is his sage mantra, and the first step to getting them feeding is a regular feeding rhythm.

"The feeding is as simple and easy as the method itself," Chris tells us. "I've got a pint of casters in a bait box by my side and I'll throw in around five or six of them for every cast."

Depthwise he starts off at around three feet, and his rig is so simple it's almost child's play.

"The blob itself sits on 3lb Preston Innovations Power Max Clear main line and right below that I position a No9 Stotz so I can keep track of the depth I'm fishing in case the blob moves," says Chris. "I also position another No9 Stotz above the hooklength when I'm fishing deeper, which I will do at the start before the fish move up in the water. The extra weight just helps the light line of my 3lb hook link break the surface and carry the bait down."

On his size 18 hook Chris presents a single caster, which needs to be falling through the water alongside the loose feed to get the fish's attention.

"The idea is to keep the feed going in little and often so that the fish start competing and move up to the source of the feed, and in the end are right under the surface." And it isn't long before that's exactly the case.

"When you start seeing them boil under the surface when the feed goes in, you know you've got them going well," smiles Chris as he shallows up, moving the two weights and the blob down to just above the hook link.

"I'll always fish at least a hooklength's depth so that the bait has a distance to fall. Sometime you'll find the better stamp of fish lurking

All you need. Blobs and Stotz with ready-tied hooks to nylon make up the rig, and a pint of casters for feed.

As simple as it gets, but loads of fun – the blob rocks!

Chris fishes just a rod length out, flicking the blob rig out without opening the bail arm on his reel.

The blob sits on the surface, but doesn't intrude into the swim so you can present bait really shallow without spooking fish.

below the smaller examples in the swim, and if you're fishing too shallow you won't be able to get down to them."

With the fish swirling and feeding hard Chris keeps the casters going in and the fish coming to the bank. The stamp of these rudd is impressive, averaging at least 8oz to 10oz – good hand-sized examples.

Although the action is frantic, what's noticeable is that Chris isn't losing many fish.

"I tend to use the larger-sized blob because its larger diameter creates a bit of resistance on the surface and with the short distance between the float and the hook this helps the hook to prick the fish before the strike, resulting in good hook-holds," explains Chris.

A couple of hours into the session the fish-a-chuck action slows and a few bigger swirls show something a bit larger has moved in. "Even

when it goes quiet you should always keep the same amount of feed going in," says Chris as he strikes into a better fish. All the feeding has attracted the lake's ide and they're a good stamp too, that validates Chris' choice of a rod and Korum CS 3000 reel for the method – this plump fish might not have made it to the net on a whip.

As the session progresses he makes a switch to double caster, attempting to increase the size

Fish The Blob

1 The Korum blob comes in two sizes and three colours, making it easier to see in different conditions.

2 To get it on your line, simply pass the main line through the wire loop the blob is supplied on in the packet…

3 …make a loop in your line to allow the blob to pass on to it easily and pull the blob over on to your main line…

4 …then pull the blob up the line and tie on your hooklength. Add a Stotz or micro shot to mark your depth.

Weird Floats

• Polaris Floats
Designed for float legering, Polaris floats use an ingenious locking system in their base that sees the float rise to the surface after casting then lock on the line when pulled against the weight of the leger to deliver bite indication.

• Dumbbell Floats
A traditional predator float, the dumbbell got its name due to its shape. It uses two buoyant balls attached via a shaft. It was used a lot on the Norfolk Broads in the 1950s and 1960s and is still used by catfish anglers today.

• Lollipops
Flat pole floats used to hold in flowing waters, these floats got their name because they look just like flat lollipop sweets. Used more on the Continent than over here they can be massive things, but highly effective in the right hands.

• Drifter
Another predator float, the drifter is used to catch the wind and sail out deadbaits to areas otherwise inaccessible to just casting alone. They require skill to use, but can produce the goods, especially on pressured waters where fish back off from casting range.

of the rudd and now roach that he's catching. It works too, with a couple of near pound-sized roach coming to the net.

"I just love this method," Chris laughs. "It's so simple that I think a lot of anglers might look down on it as an option, but it works so well. It doesn't tangle, it's easily adjustable and it's cheap – what's not to like!"

The results speak for themselves. Fishing the blob almost at his feet, feeding three-quarters of a pint of casters and having a whale of a time, Chris has put a good 30lb to 40lb of stunning rudd, roach and bonus ide on the bank in around four hours of fishing. It's a tactic that can be put into action anywhere, with silver-stuffed commercials the obvious place to give it a go. Our conclusion? If you're after a simple, fun and fish-filled day's fishing, get on the blob! ■

In a short session this is what the blob produced at Astwood Fishery – amazing stuff.

Venues

Sywell Reservoir, Northamptonshire
A day-ticket water with a rich history of tench fishing, this reservoir has produced fish well into double figures.

Frensham Great Pond, Surrey
Run by Farnham Angling Society, Frensham Great Pond is a great venue for smaller specimen tench and, on the right day, in good numbers too.

Lemington Lakes, Gloucestershire
A commercial fishery with waters offering just tench fishing, meaning it's a great venue for the budding tench angler to get some action under their belt.

Tench
Tinca tinca

The prize at the centre of a generation of mist-filled summer mornings, the tench is quite possibly the UK's most popular fish. As welcome a sight at the end of the line of the matchman as specimen and pleasure anglers alike, the olive-skinned species possesses a charm that can captivate the angler in both looks and touch. The latter, that unique sleek feel when handled, comes from the fish having small scales that are embedded in its skin.

With a large paddle tale and muscular cyprinid build the tench is also a proper scrapper, fighting hard whatever size of the species is hooked. At specimen weights this tenacity can make *Tinca tinca* a thrilling target and is a fact that has seen many big-fish anglers dedicate a large proportion of their time on the bank in pursuit of the species.

Tench can be found throughout a range of water types, from lakes and canals to slow-flowing rivers and large reservoirs, although they don't like strong flows. A bottom feeder, locating feeding tench can be made easier by their tendency to release tiny bubbles from the bottom detritus as they dig around in it for bloodworms and other insect life. As any angler who has ever fished for tench knows, seeing a patch of pinhead bubbles fizzing up next to a lily patch is one of the most exciting sights in the sport.

Over the past few decades, as with many other UK species, the size of tench being caught has exploded. In the 1970s if you caught a fish of 7lb you would have landed the fish of a lifetime. Today the target for such an achievement is a tench over double figures – a challenging weight to break, but possible in more and more waters around the country.

The Facts

Record: 15lb 3oz caught in 2001 by Darren Ward from an undisclosed southern stillwater
Max weight: 15lb+
Max length: 28 inches
Max age: 20 years
Specimen weight: 7lb
Spawn: Tench spawn based on temperature rather than a specific time of the year, needing a constant water temperature of around 18°C to get things started

Tench
the natural approach

Why try to catch tench on artificial baits, when you can tempt them with a natural alternative? Paul Smythe explains how…

Fact File
Name: Paul Smythe
Age: 42
Hometown: Newbury
Sponsors: Pallatrax, Experience Fishing

There is one fish that gives away its location when it feeds more than any other, and that's the tench. Once these fish get their heads down in the silt the surface above them comes alive with hundreds of micro bubbles. It's a sight that can give even the most experienced angler goose bumps.

Tench love to forage around for snails and other crustaceans that live in the dark matter of estate lakes and mature gravel pits, so it's some surprise that more anglers do not use natural baits more often when targeting these olive-green fish. Today anglers tend to fish more with imitation baits – fake maggots and corn being the favoured choices of many – so it was a refreshing change to meet an angler who was targeting tincas at the opposite end of the spectrum, with baits that were more natural to the fish: snails and mussels, over a feed that was also laced with smaller natural feeds such as bloodworm and daphnia, which you will find in the majority of stillwaters in the UK.

Clear Patch

I met up with specialist Paul Smythe during a session at the Carp Society's Horseshoe Lake, Gloucestershire, which, as well as having a stock of pristine carp, is home to quality tench.

Paul was there to put some of the new Pallatrax baits to the test, and had set up in the ►

The clear gap in the weeds was close enough that Paul was able to 'prebait' by hand.

far corner of the venue's Summer Bay arm – a shallower part of the pit well known for its summer tench action. The water was clear and weedy, but there were visible areas that looked weed free where the lake bed dropped off to between five to six feet. Paul reckoned that was the depth to try for the tench, and close to a bed of weed that offered plenty of cover.

And after casting around a few marks, he found a clear patch around five rod lengths out, just slightly to his left.

Dried Naturals

Before setting up his rod Paul needed to spend a little time preparing his feed for the session, as many of the ingredients he wanted to include were dried natural baits. After pouring a bag of Method mix into a large mixing bowl, he added dried bloodworm, daphnia and Gammarus shrimps plus a large helping of small, brown and black dried snails, plus some dried mussels, all from Pallatrax's Naturals and Hidra ranges of dried baits. He also added a few handfuls of pellets for good measure. Then, after adding plenty of water – agitating the mix as he poured – Paul gave the

dried ingredients time to absorb the liquid. He would return to this a few times to add more water until the sticky mix was right to wrap around his inline weight, and to check that the naturals had rehydrated. For the best results, he likes to leave the mixture for at least 30 minutes before it is ready to use – longer if necessary.

> **Once the feeding stopped it was a case of waiting for signs – it didn't take long.**

While he was preparing the feed, Paul also dropped some of the mussels and snails into a small pot of water and allowed them to soak. These he would use as his hook baits, so he left them as long as possible to fully rehydrate. Once ready they could be hair rigged on a size 12 hook.

Method-Type Setup

With such a small area to fish Paul decided on a single-rod attack and had set up a light barbel rod, which doubles nicely as a tench rod, which he used with a MAP ACF reel

loaded with 10lb mono. On the business end he had attached a free-running, inline Pallatrax Stonze weight – a natural alternative to the usual leads that many anglers use.

This was stopped with a small swivel that sat just inside the base of the weight, and on to which he tied a short hook link. It's an alternative setup for fishing the Method, as the feed is then wrapped around the weight, rather than on a flat or frame-type feeder. However, unlike when fishing with the latter, the hook bait is not buried in the feed, as with enough feed wrapped around the weight the hook link is prevented from tangling.

Prime The Swim

During the time he was setting up, Paul had been watching the water for signs of feeding tench. All had been quiet, so as the gap in the weeds was within throwing distance he decided to encourage the fish on to the spot

Paul fished an inline Pallatrax Stonze weight with a short hook link. It works by moulding the feed around the weight, Method-style. It's a tangle-free setup that creates a patch of feed when it breaks down.

by feeding three soft balls of his Method/naturals mix.

He didn't make the balls too firm, as he wanted the feed to break up as it fell, so that the particles spread out into a wider area and, with luck, some falling into or close to the edge of the weed. This he hoped would encourage the fish out from the security of the underwater forest, and out to his hook bait.

As the balls fell, you could just make out the cloud they created, which tempted one of two small fish – probably rudd – to pick off the few scraps that floated to the surface. Then once the feed had settled it was a case of watching and waiting for any telltale signs of tench.

Things went quiet for a while but then, without warning, a mass of bubbles broke the stillness, as it was clear the fish had found the feed.

A Waiting Game

Now Paul made his first cast, landing the ball of feed as close to the weed as he dared. The fish were feeding heavily enough that they took no notice of the rig falling through the ▶

It's Only Natural

1 The dry ingredients – just add water!

2 To the groundbait add dried bloodworm.

3 Next it's plenty of Gammarus shrimps.

4 A big handful of daphnia to liven up the feed.

5 Small snails – tench have a weakness for these.

6 Mix dry then add water to create a veritable feast.

Rehydrated Hookers

1 Paul soaked small brown and black snails, plus mussels, for 30 minutes.

2 A bunch of small snails proved to be the successful choice.

3 A larger brown snail gives you a bigger bait option.

4 Tench are known lovers of mussels, so give them a go.

This male fish is bigger than the average size for its sex. The rule of thumb is that the females grow to double the size, or more.

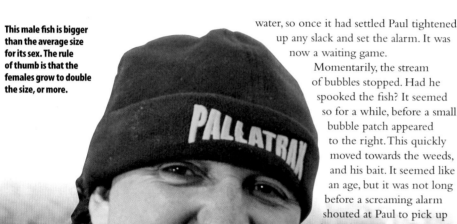

water, so once it had settled Paul tightened up any slack and set the alarm. It was now a waiting game.

Momentarily, the stream of bubbles stopped. Had he spooked the fish? It seemed so for a while, before a small bubble patch appeared to the right. This quickly moved towards the weeds, and his bait. It seemed like an age, but it was not long before a screaming alarm shouted at Paul to pick up his rod.

He indicated that the fish felt heavy, but that was due to the fact that it had bolted straight for the weed bed. It took a little persuasion but the fish finally swam back into the clear water, and, after a short battle, into Paul's net. It was not a massive specimen by Horseshoe standards, but a closer look revealed it was a male fish, which are much smaller that the females, so it was a good size for its sex.

Sadly, that proved to be the only fish of the session, as it seemed that commotion created when the tench was hooked had spooked the rest of the shoal back out into the wide expanse of the lake. However, that one fish has given food for thought when it comes to which baits to use – fake, or natural? ▪

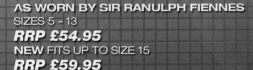

Bob's Tackle
Rod: 12ft 6in Browning
Hybrid Power Waggler
Reel: Browning Hybrid
Com FD
Main line: 6.7lb
(0.16mm) Browning
Hybrid Power Mono
Hooklength: 4lb
(0.14mm) Browning
Cenex
Hook: Size 14 Drennan
Carp Maggot

There are few better feelings for the summer angler than catching tench on waggler tackle.

Anchors aweigh!

You won't catch many tench with a waggler unless you anchor your hook bait on the bottom. Four-time world champion Bob Nudd tells you how.

Fact File
Name: Bob Nudd
Hometown: March, Cambridgeshire
Sponsors: Browning, Van den Eynde

I love fishing for tench with waggler tackle. There's something very special about watching a float, and it's even better when its orange glides beneath the surface to be greeted by a hooped rod and, a few minutes later, by a gleaming 'tinca' in the landing net.

For me, catching tench on the float is all about early summer's mornings, pinprick bubbles as a fish or two root around the bottom, and the never-give-up fight that only a hooked tench can give.

But catching tench with a waggler requires an approach that's very different from that required for most other species.

For a start, they nearly always feed hard on the bottom. This means there's no place for delicately shotted, on-the-drop rigs that I'd use for roach fishing. For tench, it's much more a case of anchoring a hook bait to the bed of the lake.

Older anglers might be aware of a technique known as the lift method, where a large shot is fixed on the line a few inches from the hook and a short, stumpy float is attached to the line with a piece of silicone rubber close to its base. Bites are usually signalled by the float tilting, lifting, or even lying flat on the surface, as a tench upends to take the bait before righting itself, thereby lifting the weight on the bottom.

My way with tench is not quite so traditional. I can't quite bring myself to fix an SSG shot three or four inches from my hook. I'm a match angler, finesse is everything to me, and an SSG near the hook doesn't show any finesse in my book!

Instead, I adopt a 'halfway-house' approach. When I'm fishing for tench, I'll always make sure that my hook bait is anchored to the bottom, but instead of using a large, cumbersome weight, I'll use a swivel with small shot if required.

The All-Important Swivel

Let me explain. I'm a big believer in attaching my main line to my hooklength with a small swivel when waggler fishing. Not only does this help prevent line spin on the retrieve, it also acts as the bottom shot on my rig.

By plumbing the depth carefully and making sure this swivel is on the bottom, I can usually ensure the rig stays put without drifting. There are times, though, when a small 12 swivel isn't heavy enough to anchor the rig. When it's windy, lakes often 'tow'. The water in them moves according to the wind. Sometimes this movement will be with the wind while sometimes it will be against the direction of the wind. The tow can vary on different parts of the lake and it will also vary according to the depth of the water and the strength of the wind.

Whatever the tow is doing, the key thing to achieve is to ensure that the rig stays put. Tench won't take a moving bait. It's easy to achieve. After plumbing the depth, move the float up the line until you know the swivel is on the bottom. Then, if the swivel is being pulled along in the tow, add a No8 shot just above it and try again. Keep adding No8s until the float sits perfectly and stays put.

Don't plumb the depth in the usual way, with

Bob's Baiting Tips

1 Casters, maggots, pellets and sweetcorn – all great tench baits for feed and hook bait.

2 Make sure that your groundbait for tench contains plenty of particles like sweetcorn.

3 Throw four balls in the general area of your float. Don't worry too much about total accuracy.

4 Loose feed pellets around your float to make some noise.

a heavy plummet attached to the hook. Instead of doing that, I squeeze an SSG shot on to the swivel joining the main line to hooklength and plumb using this.

A couple of final points to remember about waggler fishing for tench. First, your float needs to be fairly buoyant, so that it doesn't get dragged under by any surface movement in the water, and second, you don't need to fish especially fine. I use 0.16mm main line on the reel, which has a breaking strain of 6.7lb, and a hooklength of 0.14mm diameter (breaking strain of 4lb). Hook is a size 14, in my favourite red colour.

Bait For Tench

Tench are highly inquisitive and I always ensure that I make a bit of noise when baiting up for them. On weedy waters, I have been known to rake a swim to create plenty of commotion and to remove weed and stir up the bottom. All this certainly stirs up their curiosity and this noise effect also has a place in my baiting campaigns.

Create a bit of noise on and in the water, and tench are sure to investigate. If the fish then find something that stirs up their taste buds, so much the better.

Several balls of sweet and sticky groundbait will often be my opening gambit, and I always make sure it contains plenty of particles, in particular sweetcorn, casters and 4mm pellets. Tench love casters by the way – never go tenching without them!

As a general rule, I'll throw in four balls of groundbait at the start of the session, making sure they're squeezed hard so that they get down to the bottom quickly.

After that, I like to loose feed over the top. Ideally, this will be casters, but if there are lots of small fish like roach in the lake, most of these will be eaten on the way down. In this situation,

loose-fed sweetcorn would be a better option.

As far as hook baits are concerned, keep an open mind when tench fishing. I make sure that I have plenty of options, but if I was pushed to make a choice, here are my top five favourites…

01 Tail of a lobworm. This is a fantastic bait and, in my experience, always tempts the biggest fish in a shoal of tench.

02 Two or three red maggots. Tench love these, but so do other species and if your lake contains lots of small fish, you might need to go for something a bit bigger. Great for catching good numbers of medium-sized tench.

03 Sweetcorn. This is another proven winner for tench and works well on commercial fisheries. Being a highly visual bait, it works well in coloured water.

04 Double caster. I don't know what it is about casters, but I can't stress enough how much tench love them. Double caster can work when all other baits fail.

05 Red worm. Perhaps a surprising choice, but if you can get hold of some, red worms are an excellent tench bait. So chat up your local friendly horse-riding school and raid their manure heap! ■

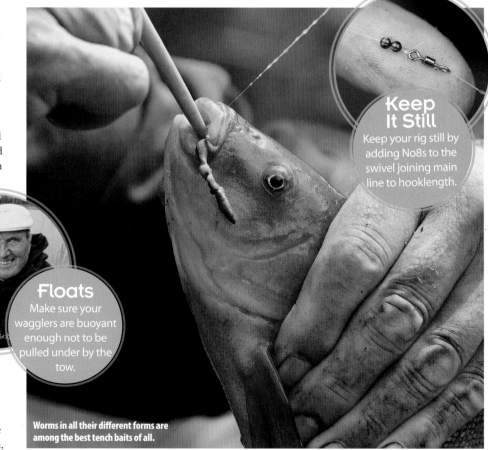

Floats
Make sure your wagglers are buoyant enough not to be pulled under by the tow.

Keep It Still
Keep your rig still by adding No8s to the swivel joining main line to hooklength.

Worms in all their different forms are among the best tench baits of all.

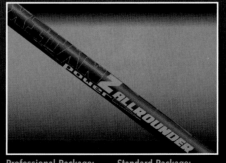

Pike
Esox lucius

The largest native, freshwater predator in the British Isles, the pike is perhaps the most recognisable of all our coarse fish species.

The power, size and ferocity of *Esox lucius* has led to its status as fish royalty, commanding a huge angling following wherever it is present. And they are present everywhere, from massive Scottish lochs, man-made trout reservoirs and Irish loughs, to the smallest rivers, drains and canals.

Stories of pike being found dead at over 80lb in the UK and Ireland, and over 100lb in the big lakes of Russia, only add fuel to the species' allure. In Britain a fish of over 20lb is a good specimen, one of over 30lb a fish of a lifetime and a specimen of over 40lb worthy of the history books.

Targeted by lures, livebait and deadbait tactics, the traditional time to fish for pike is from October through to the end of the coarse season. The timing is a mix of improved weights – female pike go on the feed from around October as they prepare their bodies for spawning – and fish conservation – cooler temperatures are better for fish recuperation following a fight. However, they can be caught year round, with lures being the preferred method during the warmer months.

Although a super-tough, highly honed predator in the water, out of the wet stuff pike are a fragile species. The highest of care is needed when handling and unhooking them, the former of which should be kept to a minimum, with the right tools for the job being a necessity.

The Facts
Record: 46lb 13oz caught by Roy Lewis from Llandegfedd Reservoir, South Wales, in 1992
Max weight: 40lb (UK)
Max length: 4¾ feet
Max age: 25 years
Specimen weight: 20lb
Spawn: Usually around March, depending on temperature

Venues

Chew Valley Lake, Somerset
A shallow trout reservoir that produces multiple 30lb-plus fish per year.

River Wye
The chance of some huge natural-water pike in stunning surroundings.

Loch Awe, Scotland
There's plenty of water to explore and the chance of some great sport north of the border.

River Thurne, Norfolk
Home to some whackers and producer of a British record in the mid-1980s.

Colour Up

Dye your deadbaits for big predator action, as Pike Pro's Jon Neafcy reveals his secrets to success.

Fact File
Name: Jon Neafcy
Age: 40
Occupation: Regional manager for a logistics company
PB pike: 35lb 1oz

A cold northeasterly bites sharper and deeper than the biggest of Esox dental work as we settle into the chosen swim of Pike Pro consultant Jon Neafcy.

Out in front a large slick of oil gives away the location of the two traps set before our arrival, with Jon vigilantly surveying the water for signs that might inform his next cast.

The venue is Manor Farm Fishing, in Bedfordshire. Primarily a carp and match venue, the complex's latest addition is a 20-year-old lake that until recently served as a nature reserve.

Over 15 acres in size, the natural water has produced pike to 28lb over the winter; although it's largely an unknown quantity, it's one Jon wants to get to grips with, and he has just the method to do it.

"It's crystal clear and freezing cold so I'm looking to get the fish feeding if they're there and give them a target to home in on," he tells us as he reaches for his bag of frozen deadbaits.

The logic of Jon's approach is straightforward. In his chosen swims he will introduce a small amount of chopped-up deadbaits, known as 'choppy'. The idea behind this is to create a haze of oils and scent in the water in a step-by-step process that should lead any pike in the area to his hook bait.

"If there's a pike in the vicinity when

Dye and scent can be added to any bait, but always take a selection because the fish might want different things on different days.

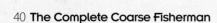

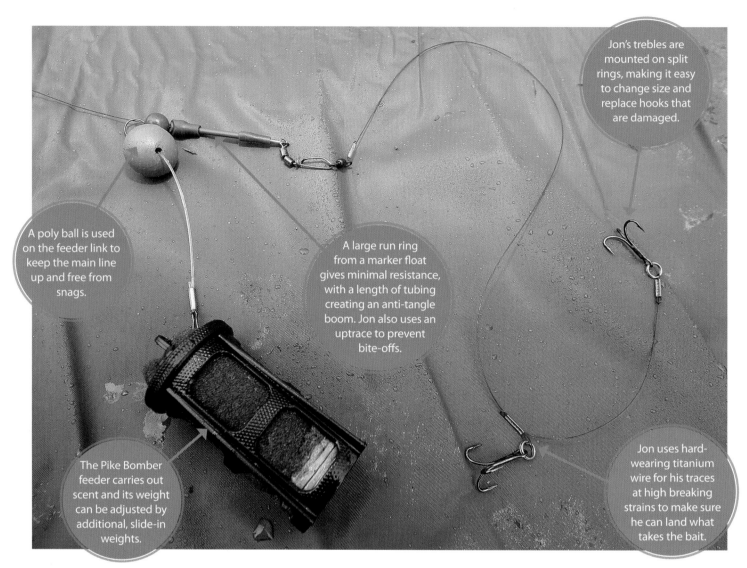

Jon's trebles are mounted on split rings, making it easy to change size and replace hooks that are damaged.

A poly ball is used on the feeder link to keep the main line up and free from snags.

A large run ring from a marker float gives minimal resistance, with a length of tubing creating an anti-tangle boom. Jon also uses an uptrace to prevent bite-offs.

The Pike Bomber feeder carries out scent and its weight can be adjusted by additional, slide-in weights.

Jon uses hard-wearing titanium wire for his traces at high breaking strains to make sure he can land what takes the bait.

the choppy goes in, the trail of oils and scent should be enough to get them interested and, even if they're fairly torpid, moving in slowly to investigate," explains Jon. "Once they find the bait, the small pieces will be inviting enough for them to take, even though their metabolism at this point will be fairly inactive. Once they do start feeding, though, that slow metabolism will speed up, leading them to want a bigger meal, and hopefully that will lead them to my hook bait. I know the choppy approach works as I've had numerous catches over it where the fish spews the fish chunks up on the unhooking mat."

Jon's choppy consists of mostly old hook baits which otherwise would have been discarded. Everything from mackerel and roach to lamprey and pollan go into the mix. Over the top of this Jon presents his hook bait, a sizeable offering that no predator could ignore.

"The pike will want a big bait that will give them a good energy return for little effort, so something like a large whole roach, pollan or herring is a good choice," says Jon as he mounts a large pollan on his hooks. "But you can give yourself a further edge if you think about colour and scent."

Slick Trick

1 The feeder is best loaded with oils by injecting them into the core via a syringe.

2 Then load up the outer layer of the feeder by pouring more over the foam.

Red For Deads

With the water being so clear in the lake, the pike will be using their keen sense of sight as well as smell to hunt prey. With this in mind, Jon prepares his hook bait so that it's as attractive as possible.

"Colouring your deadbaits can be a huge edge, especially on clear waters and when the fish are seeing a fair bit of angling pressure," Jon reveals.

The Pike Pro range includes winterised oils, dye and scented dye sprays.

Using the Pike Pro range of dyes and dye oils he quickly transforms his deadbait from just a fish into a red, oily, underwater beacon.

"As they come in a spray bottle you just squirt it on to the baits a minute or so before you need them and they're ready to go with very little fuss," says Jon. "The combined dye and oil sprays are my favourite. Once in the water they leech out around the bait like a cloud but still stay on the bait for a long time. The best I've found is the red lamprey oil, which has caught me a lot of fish. All of the dyes are also food grade, so you can rest assured if you get any from your hands to your mouth, which does happen as it can be a messy job; you'll be fine."

> **"Look for ambush points and areas that will hold a more consistant temperature. "**

When it comes to applying the dye there's no fixed pattern, with Jon colouring the entirety of his baits, just half of them or only specific patches. "It all depends what the pike want on the day really and that can apply to the colour, the oil and the amount you apply," explains Jon. "If you work one water for a while you will start to get a good idea of what the fish will be after in what conditions. Until you work out a pattern, though, you will need to ring the changes during a session and at some point, if the fish are present and feeding, you should work it out." ▸

Jon prepares to launch his bait boat loaded with choppy and deadbait.

It's best to spray the fish once they have defrosted as they then absorb the dye better.

To The Bait Boat

When it comes to bait delivery Jon has a secret weapon up his sleeve that can help with finding and utilising the type of swims he's after. "I like to use a bait boat for my piking. Firstly because my boat has a built-in fishfinder, which I use to measure depths and locate drop-offs and snags," Jon tells us. "Secondly, at range, it allows me to be much more accurate with my baiting."

This needn't put off anglers who don't own a bait boat, though. At close range the choppy can be delivered by hand, while at further range a catapult can be used. And, of course, feature finding can be done with an hour of 'leading' around your chosen swims.

After a good scout around with the bait boat, Jon has chosen his swims, opting to fish a deeper trench around a third of the way across to an island, while his second bait is boated to a hole just short of the island.

"I'm looking for ambush points and spots with more constant temperatures, especially on a relatively shallow water such as this where a northeasterly, like we have today, can really put a chill through the water. These holes offer the pike both so they're great places to try."

Think About Your Rigs

With the bait prepared and precision bombed over the target area, it's time for Jon's rigs to come into play.

"Being fairly shallow I'm straight legering on both rods today," says Jon. "If it was deeper or there was a drop-off where the line could catch and suffer abrasion problems I would be float legering."

For his straight legering Jon employs a titanium trace for his hooks and an uptrace. "An uptrace will not put any pike off taking your bait, but it could prevent you from getting a bite-off if a pike takes the bait and continues along the rig and gets the line in its jaws," he tells us. "For long-range fishing I would always use braid; however, a number of fisheries that offer carp and pike fishing don't always allow it. Because of this, today I'm using a pre-stretched mono line developed in Australia for sea anglers, and it's as close to braid as you can get."

Elsewhere on his rig Jon also has another secret weapon, a bait bomb. It's basically a specially designed cage feeder housing a foam insert loaded up with more oil, with Jon both injecting oils into its core and pouring it over the outside. "Again it's a great edge for drawing pike into the swim and getting them interested in feeding," he explains.

Feeding?

Working the area hard through finding, feeding and ringing the bait and colour changes on his new spot, Jon is tireless in his pursuit of the fish. However, as he has pointed out, working a shallow, fairly open lake when a bitterly cold northeasterly wind is sucking every degree of temperature out of the water could well see the fish unwilling to feed whatever you do. And that's how it turns out on the day.

The action culminates in a single jack grabbing a mackerel on the retrieve, a perfect row of teeth marks on one side of the bait (just off the hooks) proof that at least something is hungry.

"That's fishing for you, especially when you're after specimens," smiles Jon as he makes one last cast into the sunset. ■

Although Jon didn't catch for the cameras his track record shows that dying your baits and adding more scent can give you a real edge when it comes to catching more pike.

Deadbait tactics

• Drift float
The drift float basically acts as a small sail, carrying your deadbait suspended below and moving it with the wind. It's a great tactic for covering lots of water, but best suited to waters with a consistent depth.

• Float leger
A hybrid of float fishing and straight legering, the float leger sees your bait fished on the bottom with a lead lying behind it; this then moves up to a float, which provides the visual bite detection. This is great for deep drop-off waters that create too much of an angle for straight legering.

• Wobble
Effectively using your deadbait like a lure, the wobbling technique sees a whole deadbait mounted head first on two trebles with a slight kink in the body. The deadbait is cast out and retrieved either straight or sink-and-draw style.

Be On Your 'Metal' For Pike

Predator ace Mick Brown explains why you should never leave spoons and spinners out of your lure box.

Fact File
Name: Mick Brown
Age: 66
Occupation: Predator legend, angling guide, author and consultant
Pike PB: 35lb 2oz

The first lure I ever cast was a spinner over 50 years ago. At the time of writing, the last lure I cast was also a spinner – a Blue Fox Original Vibrax size 5. In the years between, I've cast many a spinner and caught endless pike to over 20lb along with lots of other predators too. The point being that whoever designed the spinner got it spot on.

Pike, After Dark

Spinners have properties that attract pike, and the signals they send out are unique to this type of lure. The intermittent visual flash from the rotating blade draws the pike's attention while the vibration it produces is clearly of a frequency that gets it noticed – something proved many times to me by catching pike with spinners in muddy water and even in the dark.

I'm a great fan of spinners and use them regularly, particularly in my first line of attack when approaching a swim for the first time.

Spinners originated in an age long before the development of modern materials and production processes. Around the same time another metal lure, the spoon, also appeared on the scene and, like the spinner, they are still popular today.

Spoon-Fed

There are many spoons that have stood the test of time and still exist in almost their original form. Modern processes have allowed recent models to be finished with more attractive paint finishes, which enhance their appeal.

I still use a lot of my old favourites, but in recent times I've been introduced to the Blue Fox spoons, such as the Lucius, which clearly exhibit improvements to form and attraction.

Simplified Fish Handling

Apart from the stated benefits, metal lures have a lot going for them. Beginners will find them easy to cast on suitable tackle. As they only carry one treble hook, fish handling is greatly simplified and a lot safer.

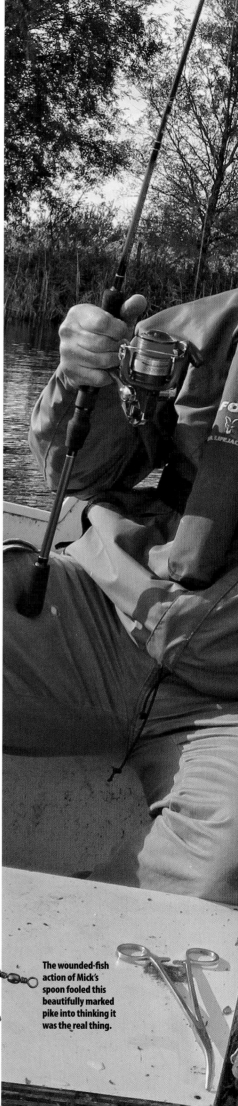

The wounded-fish action of Mick's spoon fooled this beautifully marked pike into thinking it was the real thing.

It's much easier to guide a pike into the waiting net when the only treble is in the pike's jaw. Lifting the pike from the mesh becomes a simple operation, and with a little practice it's quite easy to remove the hook with a pair of long-nosed pliers, without the worry of a second treble catching your hand.

Spinners and spoons are definitely lures I would recommend for the inexperienced or anyone wary of handling pike.

Sink Rate

As metal lures have no buoyancy, they are naturally going to sink as soon as they hit the water. This is a great way of searching different depths without having to change lures. By following a logical procedure you can search a swim from top to bottom in a very short time. There are a few general rules you must follow to make the search thorough, without catching the bottom or hanging a lure on a snag.

I like to have a range of different weights of spoons and spinners with me. Lighter models sink slowly and can be retrieved slowly, making them a good choice for shallow water. When approaching deeper water though, I reach for a heavier lure. If you're unsure of what's beneath the water, it's always advisable to start with a lighter lure, and see whether it will fish the whole water column from top to bottom.

Balance The Weight

It might be useful to detail how weights of typical lures vary and what's available. For example, the Original Vibrax spinner comes in six sizes with the smallest weighing just 3g, up to the largest weighing 18g. The Blue Fox Lucius spoon comes in four sizes from 12g up to 36g.

The rod and reel to use with these lures should have a corresponding casting weight if you're to get the best from them. As I tend to use those at the heavy end of the weight range, I look for a rod with a 10g to 30g casting weight, which for me is an 8ft Shimano Technium DF. This is perfectly balanced with a Technium 4000 FC reel, loaded with 20lb Power Pro braid.

Naturally, I use a wire trace, and have this season been experimenting with a 'Knot 2 Kinky' single-strand titanium leader. At first I was wary of its 6in length, but after catching more than 30 fish with no problems I'm happy, especially with its kink resistance and durability.

First-Cast Fish

Finding the pike's feeding depth is vital. At times they will attack at any depth, but often getting it right makes a difference between catching or not, so searching right down to the bottom is usually important. You will know that you've reached the bottom when you make connection with it, so proceed with caution by starting the ▶

Start the session by exploring the deeper water at the edge of submerged weed beds.

Cast your lure as close as possible to the bankside reeds and tweak it back to tempt a predator out of its ambush hole.

first cast with an instant retrieve.

It's surprising how many pike will hit the lure on that first cast. With each consecutive cast, allow a few extra seconds for the lure to sink deeper. When your lure catches the bottom, you need to lift the rod tip and speed up the lure to ensure you get it back.

Leisurely Retrieve

If, after several retrieves at increasing depths, you're not hitting the bottom, it's likely you need to use a heavier lure, and start the procedure again. This may seem time-consuming, but it's a good idea to take your time and not be in a rush – a leisurely retrieve often works better than a fast one, especially in cold water.

Spoons and spinners can be used at any time of the year, and should never be neglected. Even in the depths of winter they will often be my first choice, and I will run them through a swim to try and pick off any active fish, before changing to a more subtle approach.

Reed Beds And Underwater Weed

On a recent day out fishing with spoons and spinners, I found the weather to be unseasonably mild as I launched my boat on the Long Lake at the Langtoft Carp Fishery in south Lincolnshire.

Even so, the very bright sunshine and flat-calm conditions, combined with the gin-clear water, ensured that the resident pike stayed well hidden in among the reed beds and underwater weed. And after an hour of fruitless casting, it was clear that I was going to have to work hard to catch anything at all.

Hit-And-Run

Spoons and spinners are great for 'hit-and-run' fishing to quickly get to know a venue, and after working out that there was typically four feet of water above the weed, it was easy to decide which lures to use. The size 5 Vibrax spinner was perfect for the situation as was the 20g Lucius spoon, both of which produced several hits through the day.

Many other lures were tried but the pike showed little interest. They refused to take surface lures and even ignored my favourite Storm Kickin Stick with its incredible lifelike swimming action that's usually irresistible. Two pike did flash at the boat as I brought in a Rapala BX Swimmer, but were not turned on

enough to grab it. All the lures I used are proven catchers, but these difficult conditions called out for something different and the carefully worked spoons and spinners saved the day.

I'll always put my hands up when I've made a mistake. On the day I only had the spinner and spoon in one colour of each and I suspect a change of colour might have brought more fish, but in my defence, how many people carry a full colour range of every lure they take with them?

At least by identifying the winning lures, I can go back on another occasion, better prepared with a few other colours. That's the joy of fishing; the anticipation of going back and getting it right the next time. I can't wait! ∎

It's crucial to get your tackle balance right. Mick uses an 8ft Shimano Technium DF rod with 20lb Power Pro braid.

Mick uses spoons that are heavier than the stated casting weight of his rod – something he'd only do when casting short.

AERO SERIES

Aero Spin

Aero Feeder

Aero Match
(Double Handle)

Aero ... the shape of things to come

X SHIP

X AERO WRAP II

AR-C SPOOL

RRP. PRICES FROM
£199.99

Protective Line Clip   Anti-Twist Power Roller   AR-C Spool and Line Reducer

---

SHIMANO AERO SERIES - DESIGNED FOR ANGLERS WHO KNOW WHAT'S GOOD FOR THEM!

The **Aero Series** is available in **Match**, **Feeder** and **Spinning** models (each technically specified for their intended use) and feature a wide diameter oversized **AR-C spool** combined with a small compact body. **Aero Wrap II** line lay, for superb casting performance with both heavy mono and ultra fine braid, **X Ship** gearing for efficient winding performance, and a super fine front drag for confident fish-playing deliver faultless performance. With each model you get a spare spool and a line reducer (2 on the Match version) to tailor the spool capacity to suit your line choice. Aero - it's the shape of things to come.

Model	Weight (g)	S A-RB	Roller Bearing	Gear Ratio
Aero Match FA	385	3	1	5.2:1
Aero Feeder FA	340	3	1	5.8:1
Aero Spin FA	330	3	1	4.8:1

Line Capacity	
Standard Spool	200m x 10lb (0.22mm)
Shallow Spool Reducer	200m x 8lb (0.20mm)
Match Spool Reducer (Match reel only)	150m x 5lb (0.14mm)

SHIMANO
www.shimano.com

You Tube
See us on **YouTube**

f shimanofishinguk

http://www.youtube.com/shimanofishinguk

Commercial Carp

Cyprinus carpio

The most popular and regularly caught species in the UK, the carp is the backbone of modern coarse fishing.

Up to 30 years ago the species was still pretty much an enigma, hunted by a small number of hard-core specimen anglers. Then came the commercial fishery. Hard fighting, hardy and with big appetites, the carp, whether common, mirror or ghost, was the perfect fish to give anglers exciting sport for their cash.

From a few pounds to specimen sizes, commercial carp are a favourite with anglers right across the board. They have completely changed the match and pleasure angler scene and given big-fish anglers access to specimens closer to home.

One of the big appeals of commercial carp is the variety of tactics that will catch them – everything from feeder and waggler to pole and surface fishing. They're so popular in fact, that the pursuit of them has spawned a number of new tactics and tackle, including the pellet waggler and the Method feeder.

There can be few anglers in the country who have never tried their hand at catching carp at a commercial fishery, but if you're one of them, give it ago. Battling hard and feeding in numbers they can be so addictive you might just get hooked.

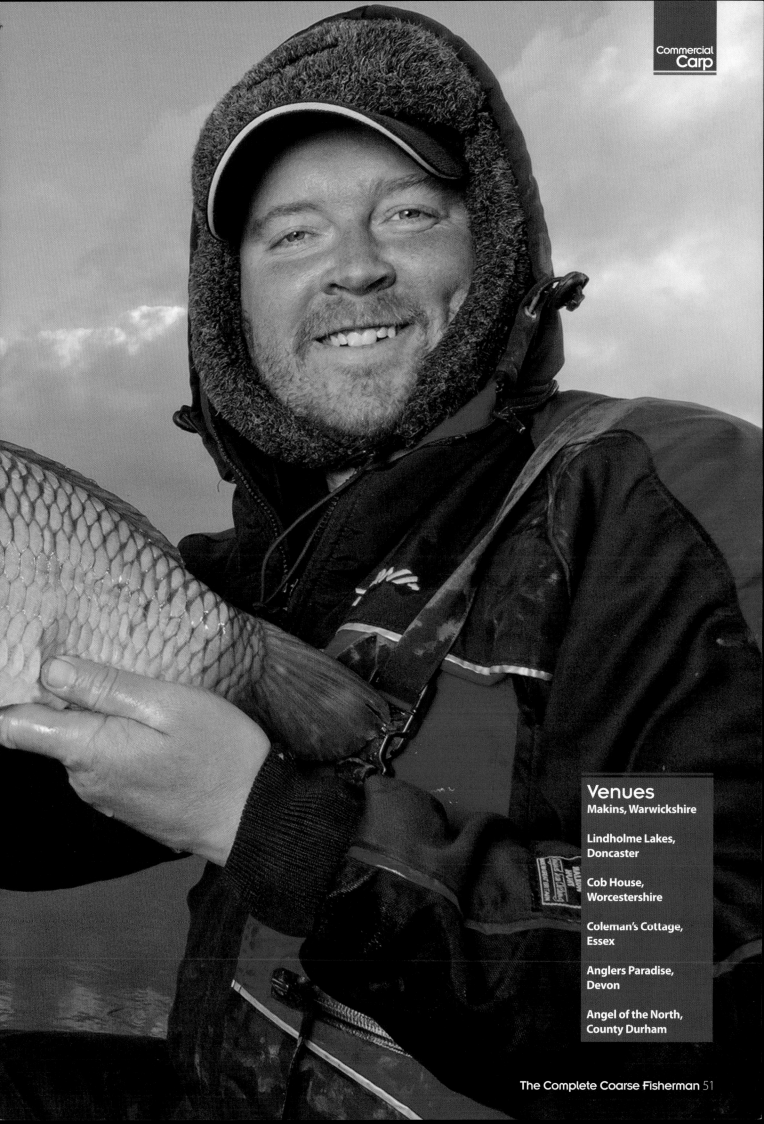

Venues
Makins, Warwickshire

Lindholme Lakes, Doncaster

Cob House, Worcestershire

Coleman's Cottage, Essex

Anglers Paradise, Devon

Angel of the North, County Durham

Think Big

Fancy getting your arm pulled by some beasts? MAP's Tony Curd reveals his approach to targeting heavyweight commercial carp.

Fact File
Name: Tony Curd
Age: 23
Occupation: Painter and decorator
CV: Multiple Fish 'O' Mania finalist

It's a fact that commercial carp are getting bigger. Gorging on barrowfuls of pellets, groundbait and boilies, they pack on the pounds almost daily, with many in fisheries around the UK now having an average weight over double figures.

There's an obvious problem with this – these bulked-up big boys fight like fury, and if you're not on the right tackle to tame them you'll be breaking off quicker then you can say: "It's only a 2lb bottom!"

The answer then is to make them the target. Weed out the goliaths from the pasty ranks on the right tackle to beat them fair and square and you'll have an elastic-stretching, arm-aching day to remember.

To guide you through the tactics, tackle and feed to put a pile of clonkers on the bank we visited the Match Lake at West Sussex's Sumners Ponds Fishery, home to some giants, to pick the brains of MAP and Bait-Tech-backed match ace Tony Curd, and it wasn't long before his arms were aching as he gave us the lowdown…

Go Long To Start

When targeting big commercial carp, for me you can't beat the pole. And my first line of attack in spring will almost always be a long-pole approach on the bottom, between 14 to 16 metres out. This puts me a good distance away from the bank, where the carp will be happier to feed early on, and is usually a banker for some early bites.

The way you feed this line is crucial in spring and although we're targeting bigger fish, that doesn't mean piling in loads of bait. This can have an adverse effect on what you're trying to achieve, bringing in a quantity of fish but not the quality we're after. Big commercial carp are clever fish and have seen it time and again; in my experience feeding for one bite at a time is a far better approach, especially early in the season.

Baitwise Bait-Tech Scopex Corn is a real favourite of mine in spring, firstly because of the visual factor in the still relatively clear water conditions of this time of year, and secondly, as the water is still cool, a lot of nuisance species will generally leave it alone. This gives me the confidence that the feed will be there until a carp moves in, making it easier to assess how to ▶

> **My first line of attack will almost always be a long-pole approach on the bottom.**

feed as the session evolves.

To keep my options open, I always like to feed two lines at this distance: one at the 10 o'clock position from my peg and another at two o'clock. One of these is fed with corn only; the other with corn and soaked 4mm pellets. Depending on the conditions I will occasionally feed the second line with just pellets, as on some days this will hold the fish for longer.

Typically I'd be looking to kick these lines off with 20 grains of corn on one line and 15 grains and a decent pinch of 4mms on the other. It's not much bait but, as I've mentioned, it's about getting one bite at a time. This would be topped up each put-in with a

Kinder pot of bait to keep things ticking over. However, if I find silvers becoming a problem due to the regular feed, I will use a big pot to introduce large quantities but less often.

My rig for fishing corn is very simple. Main line is 0.15mm to a 0.15mm hooklength carrying a size 16 B911, strong enough to land anything you're likely to hook providing there aren't many snags around. Here today we're fishing open water so I'd be confident of beating any carp using a relatively soft MAP Twin Core 10-14 elastic. My float choice is a MAP SD2 in a 4x14 size, ideal for the 4½ft-deep swim I'm fishing, shotted with a strung bulk of No9s starting from the hooklength connection, spaced upwards an inch apart – perfect for corn fishing,

but plumbing up at absolute dead depth is crucial when fishing like this.

To make sure I'm accurate I plumb my rig up twice, firstly with a very heavy 30g plummet which I use to feel around on the bottom for any obstructions or anything that may prevent the fish from feeding. Then, once I'm happy, I use a lighter plummet to get an even better reading – you'll be surprised how far out you can be sometimes on soft-bottomed commercials!

At this time of year it's also worth having a shallow rig ready to go as the fish will venture off the bottom on warmer days. Pinging meat out and fishing a hair-rigged cube on the hook can be a great way of nicking those odd big bonus fish on the same line.

At five to six metres Tony feeds just meat by hand – the key here is to keep a steady trickle going in before you fish the line, which can be the most productive of all three areas.

For real 'lumps' the margin rules. Tony primes a swim down the edge with a fairly dry groundbait mix that isn't compacted, just potted in to form a cloud and a bed for the carp to get their heads down on, usually later in a session.

A Couple Of Hours In

My second approach is the 5m to 6m line. This has been covered a lot in the past, but spring is when it starts coming into its own. Typically it starts to produce a couple of hours into a session as the big fish move towards the margins in search of more feed, and the extra depth you have by fishing at this distance is vital to the fish feeding confidently in bright daylight conditions.

To my mind there's only one bait I'd attack this swim with – meat! I like to use the Bait-Tech N-Tice Polony, a great bait that is slightly different to most luncheon meats and also contains a lot less fat, which can prove very effective for outsmarting the bigger, clued up-carp. I prepare the feed for this by using the 6mm blade on my meat cutter, but always have some 8mm pieces ready for a standout hook bait.

Feeding is very simple on this line but you need to be disciplined and keep bait going in throughout the day. I pot in around a quarter of a big pot at the start of a session and will loose feed four to five cubes every 90 seconds or so. This provides a constant trickle of bait going in, which will build the swim steadily for a couple of hours before fishing it, but before I do go in on it, the last couple of times I feed I'll increase the bait to 10 cubes to get the fish feeding properly.

Once you begin to catch at five metres it's always best to double the amount of feed you introduce. Around 10 to 12 pieces is about right to keep the fish in your swim.

Tackle for this line is a little different due to it being a 'bagging zone'. You need to be able to land fish quickly and with minimal fuss, so for this reason I use a 0.17mm main line. This gives me the option of upping my hooklength diameter should things get hectic, although I'd always start on a 0.15mm hooklength.

Floatwise I find the MAP SD4 in a 4x14 to be the best for this style, again shotted with a strung bulk of No9s and plumbed to dead depth. A size 16 B911 would be my starting hook, going up to a 14 if I needed to fish a bigger bait or I was catching a lot of fish. Elastic is also beefed up a bit to a 12-16 MAP Twin Core, which is still soft but has more power for landing fish quicker. ▶

At 14 to 16 metres Tony develops two swims – one with just corn, the other with corn and pellet – to see which the carp respond best to on the day. Don't be tempted to feed too much; this is Tony's initial feed amount.

At Your Feet Later On

The third and final method for extracting big carp from commercials is probably the most popular of all – margin fishing. Spring can be a good time of year for some great catches down the edge, with my approach revolving around groundbait. This is an unbelievable method and a superb way of attracting large carp to your peg without having too much feed there, increasing the amount of bites you get due to your hook bait being one of only a few larger food items in the swim.

When you decide to feed the margins is a very important aspect of its effectiveness. The fish don't venture close to the bank until later in the day on most venues, so there's no value in feeding it any earlier than a couple of hours in. Typically in spring I'd kick my margin lines off with three big pots of loose groundbait cupped in with just a few hook-bait samples included. For my session today I fed and fished corn, but dead maggots or meat can be very good. My favoured groundbait mix without question is Bait-Tech Karma and Bait-Tech N-Tice in a 50:50 combo.

My margin rigs all follow one common theme – strength! These big fish are only coming into the edge to feed and they aren't worried about heavy lines at all, so my rigs are made up on 0.19mm main line to a 0.17mm hooklength; strong stuff which will cope with the initial surge of power from a double-figure carp.

Float durability is also extremely important – the last thing you want is to get a swim going and have your float explode if it gets pulled through the reeds. It not only disrupts your rhythm but also wastes a lot of time when you may only have an hour's window of opportunity to make the most of the action. A MAP IS3 float in a 4x12 size shotted with a simple bulk eight inches from the hook has been spot-on today and is, without a doubt, my favourite margin float of all. A 12-16 Twin Core Hollow elastic completes my setup. ■

Big-Carp Waters

Looking to latch into some lumps to really test your elastic? Check out these top big-carp venues.

• **Drayton Reservoir**
Daventry, Northamptonshire NN11 0SG

• **Larford Lakes**
Near Stourport, Worcestershire DY13 0SQ

• **Gold Valley Lakes**
Gold Lane, Government Road, Aldershot, Hampshire GU11 2PT

• **Viaduct Fishery**
Cary Valley, Somerton, Somerset TA11 6LJ

In just a few hours using his approach on Sumners Ponds Fishery's Match Lake Tony had bagged over 60lb of carp, with these four the best – the biggest easily breaking the 12lb barrier. Great fun!

EXACTLY THE POLE YOU ALWAYS WANTED

Choose Your Own Top Kit Package

Choose Your Own Top Kit Package

Whether you prefer mostly match kits, power kits or a mix of both – by choosing any of the TKS pole range YOU CAN HAVE EXACTLY the package that suits your style of fishing. Your retailer will arrange this for you.

PTFE Bush Fitted on all Kits

After you have chosen your pole and the kit package that suits you best, they will be supplied to you with a quality PTFE bush already fitted. No more searching around for the correct size and using up your time cutting back sections and fitting them yourself – very useful !

Supplied with Tubes & Holdall

When you have chosen your new pole it would be a shame not to complete the purchase with an immaculate BRAND NEW holdall. TKS poles are supplied in a top quality holdall ! Additionally, protective tubes are included.

Reinforced Band & Joints

Many anglers these days like to use an elastic puller from the side of the section- we have reinforced the correct area on the section for the required drilling. You can leave this section untouched if you wish – the section performance will not be affected. All section joints are also reinforced, reducing wear.

Same Length Kits & True Length Design

Because TKS pole top kits are made the same length, when the pole is fitted together you don't get a pole that is a different " fishing length ". This approach means that the traditionally supplied, but not often used, number 1 sections are not needed. You also benefit from the accuracy that "same length " provides.

Mini Extension & Cupping Kit

The ultra rigid cupping kit has the adaptor already fitted - saving you time and money. Importantly, it is designed to be exactly the same length as the power and match kits giving the feeding accuracy that is needed. A reinforced Mini Extension is also included in the TKS package – a very useful extra - it fits the 13m 14.5m and 16m sections.

Standard Pole Package:

- **1 x Pre Bushed Match Kit Fitted**
- **3 x Pre Bushed Power Kits**
- Rigid Cupping Kit & Cups
- Reinforced Mini Extension

SSP £599.99

The Expert View

Pure class for the cash. If you're in the market for a 14.5 metre pole then the MAP TKS 401 must be given serious consideration. A smashing package that I suspect will even impress top-flight matchmen.

Dave Woodmansey - IYCF Editor

Standard Pole Package:

- **1 x Pre Bushed Match Kit Fitted**
- **3 x Pre Bushed Power Kits**
- **1 x Pre Bushed Match Kit**
- Rigid Cupping Kit & Cups
- Reinforced Mini Extension

SSP £699.99

For features scan here

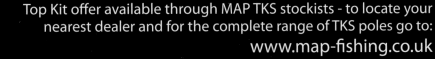

Not So Simple

The bomb-and-pellet approach is a great way of fishing your local commercial, but it's not as simple as you might think, as Maver's Andy Kinder and fishery owner Phil Briscoe explain.

Fact File
Name: Andy Kinder
Age: 43
Hometown: Sheffield
Occupation: Tackle rep
Sponsors: Maver, Marukyu

Fact File
Name: Phil Briscoe
Age: 58
Hometown: Redditch
Occupation: Managing director of Maver UK
Sponsor: Maver

Andy Kinder's bait has been in the water barely 20 seconds when the tip on his soft rod is pulled savagely towards the middle of the lake. He doesn't need to strike. The fish has hooked itself and less than a minute later, a pristine 3lb F1 lies in the net. It is a process he repeats time and again over the next three hours… and all on what appears to be the simplest of methods.

But appearances can be deceptive. Andy's bomb-and-pellet approach might not be rocket science, but try telling that to other anglers on the Match Lake at Larford Fishery, struggling for a bite only a short cast along the bank.

"Bomb-and-pellet fishing is very straightforward, but I still see anglers who don't seem to catch with it," he says. "Why? Well, I think their failure is down to one main factor – their feeding is wrong. The main thing with this method is that you have to feed constantly and you have to work out how much to feed each time. Get this right and you'll catch on almost every commercial fishery."

It's certainly an exciting way of fishing, ably demonstrated by Andy and his friend Phil Briscoe, who is fishing at the next swim. Phil, who happens to own the lakes they're fishing, is also the managing director of Maver UK. Phil

has acquired something of a reputation as an expert on the bomb and pellet, with several 100lb match hauls to his name.

Like Andy, Phil stresses the need to feed your swim in the right way. "For me, it's all about confidence. Many anglers give up on it if they haven't had a bite within 20 minutes. I'll give it an hour and a half before turning to something else."

Pleasure anglers, of course, have no such problems, and if you want some seriously exciting commercial-water action, it's certainly a method worth adding to your armoury. So how do Andy and Phil do it?

The Right Pellets
There's nothing complicated where bait is concerned. On the majority

Another big Larford F1 comes to Phil's net.

Sanagi!
Marukyu SFA 430 liquid adds weight and flavour to your pellets.

Andy shows the stamp of carp you'll catch on the bomb-and-pellet approach.

Two Bomb Setups

1 Phil prefers his bomb to be running free on the line…

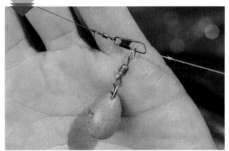

2 … while Andy prefers his to be fixed.

of commercial lakes, hard, 8mm pellets are the only feed you need. You'll either have to use the fishery's own, or your own favourite ones if you're allowed to bring them. You might need three 1kg bags for a day's session.

Phil feeds his pellets completely dry, while Andy will often add a couple of squirts of Marukyu SFA 430 sanagi liquid to his. This liquid is high in protein and especially effective when the water is warm, claims Andy – perfect, in fact, for summer and autumn work. This viscous liquid also adds weight to the pellets, so they can be fired further than dry ones. Smaller and larger pellets can be used for feed but, as a general rule, 8mms are best.

Being quite heavy, these 8mm pellets can be fired by catapult a good distance, up to 30 metres or more, depending on wind strength and direction. In fact, the distance to which they can be fired is your casting distance, so test this out first.

As far as hook baits are concerned, Andy and Phil differ slightly here. While Phil usually sticks to exactly the same pellet he's feeding, Andy takes a variety of hook baits. Included are the same pellets he's feeding, plus some Swim Stim and Robin Red from Dynamite Baits and definitely some Marukyu JPz in original red and the new Nori green.

Both anglers attach their hook pellets hair-rig style but Phil, always keen to keep things simple, uses a bait band and slides the pellet inside this. Andy, on the other hand, ties a very short length of hollow elastic (Maver Dual core 8-11 is best, he has found) to the end of the hair. This elastic ▶

Bait And Tackle Tips

1 The ideal rest – your rod won't be pulled in!

2 Make sure your reel has a free-spool facility… and use it!

3 Phil always bands his pellets.

4 Andy uses elastic to secure his hook baits.

5 Start by feeding half a dozen pellets, but increase if you need to.

is then pulled through the bait with a baiting needle. Hard pellets have to be drilled for this, but meat and JPz can be hooked simply by pulling the needle and elastic through.

Rigs

Again, there are subtle differences between our anglers. For Phil, the bomb slides along the line, stopped below by a soft bead and swivel to which the 15in hooklength is attached. Five inches above the swivel and bomb is a float stop, which prevents the bomb sliding up the line and helps create a semi-bolt-rig effect.

"I like this setup because there's absolutely no chance of a fish being left pulling the bomb around if a breakage occurs above the hooklength," he says.

Andy prefers to fix his bomb inside the link swivel to create a bolt-rig effect, stressing that he's never had a breakage as he always uses at least 10lb breaking strain main line.

It's important to use a decent-sized bomb. Obviously it needs to be heavy enough to cast to the spot easily, but it also needs to stay put so that the fish bolts when it takes the bait and feels the resistance from it. One of 15g is ideal, or a little heavier in deep water or windy conditions.

Feeding

This is what can make or break your session. Feed too many pellets, and the carp will take too long to find your hook bait; feed too few pellets, and you might not draw the fish in the first place, or they might even come up in the water to get at them before other fish do.

Today, the carp are highly active. It's hot and there are plenty of fish at the surface. For this reason, Andy and Phil decide to feed more

Hook Baits
It can pay to vary your hook baits.

pellets – a dozen or so each time – than they normally would, in a bid to get the fish down. The swims are only four feet deep, so it's a tall order, and as they fish they constantly see false bites as carp swim into the line.

Try to concentrate your feed pellets tightly, which is easier with fewer pellets in your catapult pouch. Take some spare catties too!

However, a proper bite is unmistakeable. In fact, our anglers need to be on their toes to prevent their rods being pulled into the lake. A reel with a free-spool mechanism is very handy for this sort of fishing!

The key is to vary your feeding until you get bites, and this can change during the course of a session.

Despite the weather

and the fact that the fish don't really want to feed on the bottom, both anglers amass big catches of F1s and carp in just a few hours.

If you fancy trying something a bit different from the pole or feeder, give the bomb and pellet a try next time you visit your local commercial… but don't take your eyes off your rod! ■

Tackle
For the session Andy and Phil use almost identical tackle…
Rod: Maver Reactorlite 10ft 6in two-piece multi-tip
Reel: Maver Tica Sportera 3507 free-spool, front drag
Main line: 10lb (0.22mm) Maver Jurassic
Hooklength: 0.20mm (8lb) Maver Genesis
Hook: Size 14 Maver Invincible CS20
Leger: 15g Maver Zinc Flatty or Pear

Three hours' frantic action for Phil and Andy – that's what bomb-and-pellet fishing can be like.

Chub
Leuciscus cephalus

R ain or shine, winter or summer, whatever bait, whatever tactic, if there's one species that will give you a bite, it's the chub.

Big-gobbed and with an appetite to match, the chub is one of the most widespread river fish in the UK. Because of this it's a hugely popular species with running-water anglers, whether in ounce-chublet format or barrel-shaped specimen sizes.

Present in the smallest of streams to the widest of rivers, it's a hardy shoaling species that can deliver both full keepnets and satisfying specimens to anglers in their pursuit. Plus it's become a common and welcome sight in an increasing number of commercial fisheries across the UK too.

The charm of the chub is that when many other species have shut up shop they will still feed. In the depth of winter you can count on chub to give you a pluck, and they will still be in the mood for a bit of hook-based nosh in the height of summer too. Pellets, boilies, corn, meat, bread, maggots, casters, livebait, deadbait, steak, lures… the chub is quite possibly the one species in the country that is targeted and caught on pretty much every single variety of bait you can think of.

This omnivorous nature, combined with the advent of high-protein baits going into rivers and the proliferation of signal crayfish, has led to a marked increase in the upper size of the chub too. Never have there been so many big chub caught as over the last few years. An 8lb fish is now the target for the serious big chub angler, whereas a few decades back a 5lb specimen was a fish of a lifetime – a record breaker could only be just around the corner.

The Facts
Record: 9lb 5oz caught from a stillwater in 2007
Max weight: 10lb
Max length: 23 inches
Max age: 15 years
Specimen weight: 5lb

Venues

Throop, Dorset Stour, Dorset
A famous stretch of the Stour, Throop can produce huge chub year round for the price of a day ticket.

Docklow Pools, Herefordshire
A stillwater venue home to large numbers of chub that are great fun to catch on a number of tactics.

Barton Court Fishery, River Kennet, Berkshire
A picturesque stretch of the Kennet containing a number of large chub. Coarse fishing in winter only.

Wag For Chub

Darren Cox beats the elements to target stillwater chub, revealing his secrets as he goes.

Fact File
Name: Darren Cox
Age: 46
Occupation: Garbolino UK general manager

I f ever I had to rely on catching one fish in the cold it would probably be a chub. Whether it's on rivers, canals or lakes, they may not be the easiest fish to catch, whatever the weather, but they are often the most willing to feed.

Today at the wonderful Docklow Pools complex the spring weather has turned the clock back a few months and subjected us to some arctic conditions… as if we haven't had enough last winter!

Thankfully my charge today is to catch some chub on the waggler and as long as I can counter the horrible gusts with the right bait and rigs then I should be able to tempt a few.

Chub are usually very active fish; they spend a lot of their time swimming around and are happy to feed on the surface when it's warm, or in mid-water and on the bottom when it's colder. The fact that they're so active is probably the reason they need to feed in most conditions, so as long as you're fishing where there's likely to be some chub and you make sure you cover your options correctly, you should manage to catch some.

> **Presentation is key. If the float's dragging through off-line or against the tow there's no chance of a bite.**

They rely a lot on sight to feed, especially in cold, clear water. The lake today is still relatively clear, coming out of a cold winter into spring, so feeding's going to be key. I've a few bait options with me, including corn and hemp, but because the water's clear I'm convinced that maggots and casters will be the best option. In an ideal world I'd like to feed maggots and fish them on the hook, but unfortunately the wind is slightly across and at me making it extremely difficult to feed accurately.

A swap to casters makes it a little easier to be more accurate. The casters are heavier, which means I can just get them close enough to the island I'm targeting. This way I can swap between maggots and casters on the hook. My choice of catapult is also very important. I've ended up having to fish my Drennan Feederpult with a long, strong, black latex elastic and moulded-mesh pouch. This is normally reserved for firing pellets a long way in bad conditions but today it is proving invaluable as it's the only one that will get my bait out accurately – that's why I always carry a good selection of catapults.

I start off by feeding 10 to 12 casters every cast to try and attract the chub to both the noise and the visual lure of the bait constantly ▶

To make the most out of a stillwater chub swim an angler has to work hard. A constant stream of 'little and often' feeding will get them interested and on the feed, while casting around the edge of your swim will pick off spooky fish.

Treating the line with a blast of line sink on your spool will help you get closer to your target, especially in windy conditions. Breaking the water's surface will mean you don't have to pull back on the float as much to sink the line, leaving your float closer to where you originally cast it.

falling through the water – the objective being to keep them in one spot anticipating feed arriving. It's really important to feed consistently every few minutes, minimum. This is the only way to build a swim, especially on cold days as you can feed sparingly but very regularly without fear of overfeeding.

My rod is a 13ft Garbolino G-System Waggler in the Power version, ideal for quick line pickup on the strike, still forgiving enough, yet with the power in the middle section to keep the chub out of the debris around the island. My Shimano Aero Match reel is filled with 3lb Maxima, a great robust line which sinks well when required. I've tried every line on the market but I just keep coming back to Maxima for reliability and durability.

My setup is fairly simple. I like the Drennan Crystal Floats in clear water for active fish as

I'm sure the clear floats spook the fish less and fish perfectly. I balance the floats up with solder wire around the base, which means I don't need to use big shot on the line that could potentially weaken it. I lock the float with Grippa stops and add a couple of No8 shot below the bottom Grippa, which prevents the float from moving on the cast. The only other shot on the line are a few No10s spread out in the four feet of water.

Drennan Wide Gape Pellet hooks in sizes 18 and 20 are perfect for both casters and maggots. They're strong enough and extremely sharp, very important when using casters and maggots to get a clean hook-hold and not burst the bait when hooking it. Garbolino G Line in 0.10mm or 0.12mm is the ideal hooklength. Dropping down in hook size and line diameter will certainly get you more bites in very clear

water but it's a fine balance between getting a bite and making sure you get the fish out. I also use a small size 22 swivel to reduce twists in the hooklength when fishing double baits. It also acts as my last shot.

To ensure the rig works even more effectively, giving better presentation, I regularly treat the line with G-Sink as it means that you don't have to manually sink the line as violently as you do with untreated line. This means that you can keep the float tighter to the island shelf where the fish are laid up rather than drag it away while sinking the line.

If the float's not holding correctly in the swim I won't hesitate to swap to a bigger one to make it sit correctly. If it's dragging through offline or against the tow there's no chance of a bite. This is an extremely important point when fishing the waggler, as you must try to pick

Islands and other cover offering features are a good draw to chub but remember to fish slightly away from them to start with, giving fish somewhere to back off to through the session.

Darren's float is weighted with fuse wire; the additional shot are used to help it pick up the tow.

Little and often is key. Casters could be fed more accurately in the wind.

Strong, sharp hooks and good-quality, light hook links were the order of the day.

Darren takes a number of different wagglers for the task, but it's the crystals he favours in clear water.

up the tow rather than the wind. When your loose feed lands in the water it will fall in the direction of the tow. If your hook bait's going the opposite way then what do you think the response from fish will be?

Get your line between the float and rod tip under the water, away from the wind's skim and make sure you have a big enough float on, and maybe even a small bulk at mid-depth, and you should be able to pick up that all-important tow. The tow has really helped me today as although the wind was howling from right to left my float was tracking the opposite way and sitting well. In fact, I could actually tell when I was going to get a bite!

Today the bites started to come fairly quickly once the feed started going in, but what was noticeable was that I couldn't get two bites in the same place. At first I thought this was

because of the wind and the fact that I was struggling to keep my loose feed in the same spot every time. But then I realised that the chub were actually very spooky and backing off from where I was casting regularly.

This signalled an important message – I had to utilise the whole swim and cast around trying to find a bite. It was important to keep the loose feed going in the same spot every time, but to fish around the feed. The chub were obviously backing off to a safe place, which is often away from where the float keeps landing. They wanted to feed and stay close to where the loose feed was, but were picking off the stray casters or maggots that were pinging off to the left or right.

These are the areas where you can usually generate a bite when you need one. Don't exploit these spots for too long and they will ▸

always be good to you. It's common to have to chase the fish around the swim, as they back off the more they're fished for. They also have a habit of moving tighter to cover or islands so it always pays to start a few metres off the islands or reeds as you will inevitably end up tight to them by the end of the session.

By far the best hook bait for me today was either double or single red maggot. I caught on all colours as well as casters, but reds complemented my feed of casters without having to change my hook bait every cast.

Today's session was extremely hard work but very rewarding, and it's very satisfying to know that I have beaten the elements.

Sessions like this are all about getting things spot-on as often as you can – get the cast right and you know a bite is imminent. Don't be satisfied if you feel you've cast in the wrong place, but do make sure you exploit all your swim. Fight the wind and the conditions and get your float where you need it and you will get a bite! However, you will only get that bite if you are accurate enough with your feeding – this is as important as the cast. Get all those elements right and you will have a great day.

Stillwater Chubbing

Fancy targeting stillwater chub? Check out these venues and get cracking.

• Rolf's Lake Fishery
Waterperry Road, Holton, Oxfordshire
OX33 1PW
Find out more: rolfslake.com

• Coppice Lane Pools
Coppice Lane, Hammerwich, near Lichfield,
West Midlands WS7 0LB
Find out more: coppicelanefishery.co.uk

• Buttler's Hill
Great Rollright, near Chipping Norton,
Oxfordshire OX7 5SJ
Find out more: 01608 684319

• Mill Road Lakes
Mill Road, Addlethorpe, Lincolnshire
PE24 4TE
Find out more: millroadfishinglakes.com

A fine net of chub and a few skimmers, on a tough, cold and windy day for Darren.

Q&A River Special

Total Coarse Fishing's Steve Martin joins Shakespeare's James Robbins for a June 16th river session where he has the answers to some burning float fishing issues.

Fact File
Name: James Robbins
Age: 39
Hometown: Kenilworth
Sponsors: Shakespeare
PB chub: 6lb 2oz

There is still something special about the opening day of the new river season. The early morning start – you cannot do that on a commercial, the sense of anticipation as to what's to come, and the stunning scenery like in our opening shot. What a swim! It's the Luddington stretch of the Warwickshire Avon, which is a wonderful stretch for fishing the float – stick or waggler. It's also one of Shakespeare-backed James Robbins' favourite waters, so Total Coarse Fishing joined him for an early morning start, with chub the main target.

And as we get loads of reader's questions asking for help on float fishing our rivers – stick or waggler, shotting patterns, float selection, and so on, we asked him about how he tackles an early season day on the bank.

Steve Martin: *Okay James, I see you've set up both a stick-float rod and a waggler. That leads nicely into the regular questions we get in the office: When do you fish the waggler or the stick float?*

James Robbins: The first thing to consider is the swim you choose. Certainly in the early part of the season when the river is slow and clear it pays to target the shallow, fast water that offers cover (shade) where the fish feel safe. If you look at my far bank here today, you will see what I mean.

SM: It's a great-looking swim. However, the water is quite clear – I'd have thought the river would have been carrying more colour after all that rain over the weekend. Will this make a difference to your tactics?

JR: No not today, as there's a slight breeze, which will help, and I will be looking to catch 30 yards below me. I've set myself up on a 'beach', below the high bank, so by keeping a low profile I'm less likely to spook the fish.

SM: Sorry, I digressed from the original question, so stick or waggler?

JR: It very much depends on depth and pace. Also, what the conditions are like. If it's flat calm then I prefer the stick, as it allows me the best presentation and control of the float. However, if I'm going to fish further across – over four rod lengths out, or in windy conditions, say – then the waggler is best. I will say, though, that whatever the conditions the waggler is a better choice for the newcomer to fishing the river. It allows you to fish baits on the drop and shallow for chub when they are feeding up in the water.

SM: What about the style of floats you'd use?

JR: On the stick-float front, I have three

Is there anything better than catching chub on the float on the first day of the new season? James Robbins would rather do nothing else!

James' Top Floats

Depending on the venue and conditions James will chose either a wire-stemmed, cane or lignum stick, or an insert or straight waggler of different lengths and thicknesses.

James' Feeding Tactics

1 James will feed up to three times every cast during the session.

2 He'll feed heavily at the start to get the fishes' attention…

3 … but will adjust the amount he feeds according to how the fish are feeding.

---

favourite types: wire-stemmed, cane and lignum. The first I would use on shallow, fast swims and it's my choice for today. The cane is an ideal float when targeting roach on slower-flowing stretches. It allows you to fish with a little finesse and is spot-on when fishing baits on the drop. The latter of the three I would use when fishing deeper water, further out. It offers a better degree of control compared to the cane types.

SM: *And wagglers?*

JR: There are two main styles – insert and straight – but these come in all lengths and sizes, so it's important to pick the right one, whichever style. I'll fish an insert waggler on slow-flowing rivers when I need a sensitive presentation for shy-biting roach. Then depending on the depth, I might pick a short, thin float or a longer, thicker model.

The straight types are all-round floats that are great for tripping baits along the bottom and overdepth. The shorter, dumpy ones are my choice for shallow glides, but when it comes to deeper swims, a long, chunky style is my pick, as it can take a large shotting capacity to get the bait down quickly.

SM: *What about shotting patterns? Are there any hard-and-fast rules when it comes to shot size and how you attach it?*

JR: How long have you got? There are some pretty basic patterns that work on most rivers, each depends on what you are fishing for. Let me start with stick floats – I fish models ranging from 3No4 to 16No4, and prefer to use only No8 and No10 shot. These are legal lead shot, which are smaller than the alternatives for the weight, and are easier to adjust on the line.

When exploring the swim for the first time I like to spread my shot out down the line, starting from 6in below the float to the hook link. This allows the bait to fall through the water slowly as it travels and gives an indication as to the depth the fish are feeding.

In deep-water swims I'll still use a spread-out pattern, but will place the first shot halfway down the rig. This has two effects. Firstly it gets the baits down quickly and the second, it pulls the rig down through small, nuisance fish in the upper layers.

SM: *Those sound like they are more geared for slower-paced waters. What about faster flows?*

JR: That's when the higher-capacity float comes into its own. I'll still use No8 shot, but I'll attach the bulk between two and three feet from the hook, depending on the depth, and then add two or three droppers. It's a setup that I would use when fishing for chub and barbel on the deck.

SM: *That seems to cover all depths and speeds of venues. Are there any other patterns that you might fish?*

JR: There is one more. I'll call it the reverse-shot setup. This is a pattern I would use if I wanted to target fish in the upper levels, but I needed to cast further out to get to them. The majority of the shot would be set closer to the float – still spread out, but the nearer to the hook the more distance there is between each shot, so once the float settles the second half of the rig will fall slowly through the water.

SM: *That's quite a choice for the stick. What about the waggler?*

JR: I fish the same way with both the insert and the straight. The bulk of my shot is set around the float, with most of it attached below. Then I would have a spread out set of five No8s and two No10s down the line. The No8s below the float can be moved down to increase the rate of descent, and/or create a bulk if need be.

SM: *Before we move on to the fishing, I'd like to ask about rods and reels, as we get many enquiries about them, length of rod especially. What's your view on this?*

JR: A good 13ft rod is ideal for most stick and waggler fishing, as long as where you are fishing is not too wide or too deep. Then a longer rod is useful. However, I wouldn't try and fish a waggler float on a rod longer than 15 feet, as it's not easy to control. If I have to fish with a rod of 15 feet or more, then I would use a stick float, or a Bolo float (that's a big-bodied, pole-type float that they use a lot in Europe). On really wide and or deep venues, then I would consider a 17ft model.

SM: *And your choice of reel(s)?*

JR: Sorry, but it's time for some product talk! If I'm fishing for small fish like dace then I would use a closed-face reel like the ABU 506 MkII. It's great for casting light floats with the weight set for on the drop fishing, but it's not man enough when it comes to bigger fish and stronger rigs. So for a lot of my fishing I use a Shakespeare Mach 3XT 035 fixed-spool model. I like to use the front-drag-type reel, as it is a more compact tool and I find the drag system is smooth to use. I can set the drag quite light, which allows more control on lighter lines when playing a better fish.

SM: *Chub are your main quarry today, so I assume that you will be fishing for them close to the deck in the clear water?*

JR: I think they will be resting under those far-bank trees, so I will be trying to gain their confidence to come out and chase the bait. So yes, I believe they will be keeping low.

SM: *Will you fish dead depth at the start or off the bottom?*

JR: As the contours of the riverbed are uneven, then I will fish just off the bottom, two inches or so, so that I can search for any downstream snags like weed and a change in depth. What I'm looking for is a nice

James' Gear
Rod: Shakespeare 13ft Mach 3 XT
Reel: Shakespeare 035 Mach 3 XT
Main line: Berkley XWR 0.16mm
Hook line: Berkley XWR 0.08mm to 0.14mm
Hooks: Size 18, 20 or 22 B520
Shot: Ignesti No8 and No10

clear run through, where I may trip over the odd change in depth, but mostly just off bottom. It's the same for both types of float.

SM: *Would you deliberately fish overdepth?*

JR: Often I will with a stick float, as it allows me to hold it back slightly against the flow, but still keep it close to the bottom, where it wafts around in the final few inches.

With regards to the waggler, there are some venues where you can fish up to two feet overdepth for barbel and bream, but for this to work you have to undershot the float so that its buoyancy pulls it along. A big chunky, thick-topped float is ideal.

SM: *What about baits for the early season?*

JR: For me there are only two options for the float: casters and maggots. I'll start any session feeding casters with hemp, and then fish a single or double bait on the hook.

If the casters don't work, then I'll switch to bronze or red maggots. I will fish one, two or even three on the hook. They all work. If it's a single bait, I'll fish a size 20 or 22 B520, two or more maggots a size 18 B520. I'll stop feeding the hemp and casters and feed just maggots. ■

Stick or waggler? Get the choice right and you can catch chub like James' Warwickshire Avon fish from your local river.

THE NEW
AGILITY
REAR & FRONT DRAG REELS

PRECISION PERFORMANCE

Exceed your expectations

The Agility reel range is designed for UK match and coarse fishing. The modern aggressive styling is equally matched by precision engineering to deliver one of the most outstanding (and stand out) reel ranges in the UK.

AGILITY REAR DRAG
Available in 35 & 40 sizes

AGILITY FRONT DRAG
Available in 35 & 40 sizes

Both Models Feature:

- 6 + 1 bearings
- Robust Stainless Steel hardware and gearing
- Anodised aluminium spool
- Lightweight Graphite body
- Positive Sure Click bail
- Anti-Twist titanium coated line roller
- Smooth multi-disc drag system
- One way clutch with instant anti-reverse
- Supplied with both single and double handle
- All reel supplied with spare aluminum spool,
  so you get 1 x shallow, 1 x deep (both aluminum)

2 x Aluminium Spool

Anti-twist Line Roller

Smooth Multi-disc Drag

And finally! With an angling heritage of over 100 years, Shakespeare prides itself on the quality and value of it's products. The Agility Front and Rear drag reel range has been designed in the UK at our Redditch headquarters and made in our own factory, that's why you'll not see the same reel from other manufacturers. Featuring high quality specifications that have been thoroughly tested, combined with superb build quality and styling, for the money we are proud to say that we don't think you can get any better. In fact for the price of similar specification reels from other companies, you can get two Agilities for the price of one!

Shakespeare®
SINCE 1897
Best Way To Fish!

facebook.com/Shakespeare.UK

ShakespeareFishingTV

YouTube

Bream

Abramis brama

The tip fisherman's dream, the specimen hunter's infuriation and the carp angler's nemesis, the bream is a multifaceted fish. Present in most waters, it is a shoaling species, roaming around in great numbers in search of food almost like herds of grazing cattle – they particularly love bloodworm beds to feed over.

Starting off at 'skimmers' (bream of under around 4lb) the bronze bream, to give it its full title, then grows into the biggest species of freshwater bream in the British Isles.

In specimen circles the target for a big bream is double figures, however, they will grow to twice that size, with the British Record well in excess of the 20lb mark – a staggering fish made fat on carpers' high-protein bait offerings. For pleasure anglers a fish of 5lb or more is a very welcome sight, and once you catch one there's every likelihood there will be more of the same size in your swim.

Whatever you call them – slabs, snotters, brasems, skimbobs – for the pleasure angler the best thing about targeting bream is that they're not all that smart or fussy, unlike some other species. The main criteria to stop, hold and plunder a marauding shoal is to lay down a good meal for them and, in the most part, that means groundbait.

Feeding groundbait, delivered through a swimfeeder and monitored from a bankside quivertip setup is synonymous with bream fishing. Fishmeal should form the base of the feed, the old slabs love it.

Get a good shoal going and you could be in for a day to remember. Bream average a much better size than other silver fish, meaning you can put a hefty weight together over a session if you get it right.

The target for most would be 100lb of bream, an awesome experience and one every red-blooded angler should aim to do once in their fishing career.

Venues

Bluebell Lakes, Oundle, Northants
In among the carp are some huge bream that run way into upper-double weights.

River Thames, Marlow, Buckinghamshire
A slow, wide and deep stretch of the river holding good shoals of bream with bags taken to over 100lb.

Ardleigh Reservoir, Essex
Good shoals of bream with some specimens among them.

The Facts
Record: 22lb 11oz
Max weight: 25lb
Max length: 80 centimetres
Specimen weight: 10lb
Spawn: April to June depending on temperatures

Feed
And The Fish Will Come

Five-time world champion Alan Scotthorne is in a positive mood as he targets deep-water skimmers on long-pole tactics.

Fact File
Name: Alan Scotthorne
Hometown: Rotherham
Sponsors: Drennan, Sensas

Skimmers and bigger bream are often the first species to wake up after the chills of winter. They regularly dominate early spring catches on commercial venues when the carp have yet to spread out, especially in deep-water pools. These fish need to put on weight before the breeding season, so it's also the time to increase the feed.

We joined current England international and record five-time world champion Alan Scotthorne for a feed-and-fish masterclass, using deep-water pole tactics at Hayfield Lakes in South Yorkshire.

Positive Rigs

On close inspection of Alan's two rigs, some observers may have been a little surprised at the size of the floats he had selected for the session. On the first rig, the lighter, he had fixed a 1.5g Drennan G-Tip 3 float, and on the other, a heavier 2g G-Tip 3. Both were on 0.14mm rig line, which, he explained, allowed him to fish a stable but positive setup. Then, rather than attach a bulk of small shot, Alan had

fixed on a 1.25g and 1.75g olivette respectively, 60 centimetres from the hook, commenting that he preferred to use the big weights when fishing larger floats. Also, when fishing deep-water pegs, it enabled him to get the bait down quickly to the bottom, where the fish were feeding.

Each rig then had three No8 droppers set equidistant between the olivette and the top of his 21cm hook link, so that the hook bait would fall at a more natural pace as it dropped through the final few feet of water. Hooks for the day were the Drennan Silverfish Maggot pattern, in sizes 18 and 16.

Flat Spot

With skimmers the main goal, Alan set about the task of plumbing up. He explained that, when targeting skimmers, you need to find a flat bottom, as the fish prefer to graze these areas rather than a steep slope, so it pays to spend a little time until you find the right spot. On some venues this can be at the bottom of a shelf on a short-pole line, but on others, like Hayfield's Adams Lake, which has a gradual slope, you may have to look a little further out. On this occasion, Alan found his ideal mark at around 13 metres.▸

Shotting Tip

Having found the depth, Alan needed to finish setting his rigs, so that each gave a positive bite indication. Many anglers would do this by adding any extra micro shot below the olivette. Alan, however, placed his 'trimming' shot about six inches above his bulk. This, he explained, allowed him to move the olivette up or down the line without having to move the shot, and when fishing deeper water – there was 10 feet in front of him – there was less chance of any tangles.

About Expanders

Hook baits for the session were to be 4mm and 6mm expander pellets, and, as a regular to the venue, Alan had discovered that the fish had started to shy off the usual 4mm baits, and he was now catching more skimmers on the bigger baits. Fishing them also had an added advantage that they were quite selective, as they helped to avoid being pestered by small fish, but were a mouthful for bigger fish like carp and bigger bream. He would still fish a 4mm bait as a change if bites slowed or he got bites from smaller skimmers that just nosed the bigger baits around.

> **The float dipped and, rather than strike into the fish, Alan gently lifted his pole.**

Alan also had his own way of preparing the hookers. Firstly, he liked to prepare both sizes of pellets at the same time. He would pump the baits in water at home the evening before, leaving them to soak for a minute before draining them and leaving them overnight. Then, once at his peg, he would pump them again using venue water, leaving them to soak for another minute before draining and placing them, ready for use, in a bait tub.

The Feed Fix

During the colder months Alan would feed softened 4mm carp pellets, but as the water warms he starts to feed groundbait as well. For this session he had mixed half a bag of Sensas Crazy Bait Gold and half a bag of Sensas Lake to give a soft mix that would break down just as it hit the lake bed.

To soften his hard pellets, Alan explained that he covered them with water for 60 seconds, drained them, and left them to absorb the water while he set up. He added that leaving the pellets to soak for too long would see them turn to mush. The quickly dampened particles sank rapidly and gave grubbing fish something to grab their attention.

Feeding Thoughts

To start the session, Alan fed two balls of groundbait plus half a pot of feed pellets. These were fed just shy of his actual line of attack, so that the feed brought the fish right into his swim. He explained that many anglers fed right over their pole line, but if the feed did land on a slight slope it could roll away from the hook bait and, in theory, pull the fish off line. Feeding that little bit shorter ensured that the fish would come in and feed in and around the rig.

Alan also pointed out that it was the same when loose feeding. It's key to fire the pellets so that they land just shy, or at worst over the top of the float. Firing too many pellets past the float would again pull the fish out and away from the hook bait. To ensure he hits the target every time, Alan shortens his catty elastic so that when it is at full stretch and the pouch is released, the feed lands in the right place. He commented that it was best to try and modify your catapults on the bank when fishing a pleasure session to save time later if you are likely to fish a match.

Lift, Don't Strike

Starting the session on the lighter of his two rigs with 4mm baits on the hook it was clear that Alan wanted to attack the swim, because as soon ▶

Lift into the fish when fishing softbaits.

Alan's catapult elastic is shortened to ensure he feeds no further than his float.

Alan fed two of these on every put-in.

Accurate feeding ensured the fish were kept close to Alan's hook bait.

Alan's Gear

Pole: Drennan Acolyte.

Floats: Drennan 1.5g and 2g G-Tip 3

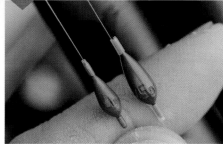

Olivettes: 1.25g and 1.75g Drennan inlines

Hooks: Size 16 and 18 Drennan Silverfish Maggot

Elastic: Drennan Green Carp Bungee (6 to 8)

Rig line: 0.14mm Drennan Supplex
Hook link: 0.11mm Drennan Double Strength

as his float had settled he fired two lots of feed pellets. You could now see his reasoning behind the use of a shortened catapult elastic, as the pellets landed on top of and just short of the float.

As the particles fell through the water, he lifted and dropped the rig to impart a little movement in his hook bait to give the impression it was part of the loose feed. He then repeated the action (without feeding), allowing the pellet to settle. It wasn't long before the float dipped and, rather than strike into the fish, Alan simply lifted his pole tip and allowed the weight of the fish against the tension of his green hollow elastic to set the hook. He pointed out that as the hook baits are so soft, very little pressure was needed to connect with the fish.

Bigger And Better

The initial run of fish were all small 'blades', so to try and catch a better stamp Alan switched to his heavier rig with a bigger bait. Then, after a few tentative indications, the float dipped and the green elastic stretched out as a bigger fish tore off out towards the middle of the pool. That initial run lasted moments, before the fish was turned. The elastic gave away the telltale 'donk' of a better bream, which, after a few minutes of resistance, was safely netted.

Alan decided to stick with the bigger bait, which was definitely the tactic for the larger skimmers. However, after catching another bigger fish the bites slowed for a while, as if the smaller fish has been bullied out of the way by the bream. Rather than potting in more feed Alan continued to loose feed, which soon pulled the fish back on line.

Alan's Edge

1 Fixing his 'trimming' shot above the olivette allowed Alan to move the bulk weight without any hassle.

2 The 6mm baits were double the size of the smaller hookers, making them irresistible to the bigger bream.

It was clear that Alan's positive feed tactics were the key to his 30lb-plus haul of silvers, as other anglers on the lake, who were not feeding, had only a few fish during the same period. He did, however, emphasise once again the importance of keeping the feed from going beyond the float so that the fish fed close to the hook bait, especially as they tended to back off once in a while. ∎

Expander Extras

When pumping expander pellets, ensure all of the baits have sunk before transferring them to a bait tub.

• To make jelly pellets, add gelatine to the liquid you use, let them soak for 30 minutes before draining and leave in the fridge overnight to set.

• Add extra colour and/or flavour to your pumped pellets by adding water-based additives to the water before pumping. For the best results, pump the hook baits three of four times.

• You don't need to prepare too many hookers for a day's fishing, so why not pump two sizes at the same time?

• If your pumped expanders float after preparation, lightly squeeze them in water before use to make them sink.

A Ton of Memories

Russ Evans takes us down memory lane to one of the most beautiful estate lakes in the land… and bags up in style!

Fact File

Name: Russ Evans
Age: 51
Occupation: Match manager for Tackle Fanatics
Sponsors: Middy and Sonubaits

Picturesque, teeming with quality fish and his place of work for nearly six years – it's no wonder Bury Hill is the destination for Russ Evans' latest fishing session.

Nestled in the green folds of Surrey, when TCF arrives at the fishery the Middy and Sonubaits-backed all-rounder has already settled into a swim, and the bend in his rod signals he's found the fish too – and not for the first time.

"This is a very special place for me, for a number of reasons," begins Russ as he makes another cast. "Back in the mid-1980s it gave me my first 100lb of English bream. In those days I was sitting on an old wicker basket and using a totally inadequate DAM 9ft Winklepicker rod, combined with a Mitchell Match reel loaded with 4lb Maxima.

"On that day I couldn't cast too far out as the rod was bouncing all over the place with

Russ' Modern Equivalent
Rod: Middy 4G Baggin Feeder
Reel: Shimano Stradic
Line: 4.2lb Middy Lo-Viz

Russ' Classic Setup
Rod: DAM 9ft Winklepicker
Reel: Mitchell Match
Line: Maxima

Accuracy is key to keeping a bream shoal feeding, with Russ' casting being clinical.

Groundbait is riddled to maximise the cloud the feeder produces as it sinks.

Russ goes for a dark mix to give the feeding fish confidence as they move over it.

its soft top section, but it didn't matter as my tip just kept pulling round."

It was a seminal day for a young Russ, who following the triple-figure haul embraced the method that, up to that point, hadn't appealed to him.

"Back then it was all a bit basic," laughs Russ. "My terminal tackle consisted of a medium-sized, plastic, open-ended groundbait feeder and 3ft tail down to a size 14 forged hook with three red maggots, while my groundbait mix was mainly brown crumb and almond food flavouring, which the bream loved and still works well today."

Times change, though, and for today's session – which sees an overcast sky and a cold breeze setting the scene – Russ' setup is far more professional.

"The old gear has gone," smiles Russ. "I'm now sitting on an all-singing, all-dancing Milo seatbox with attachments and using a Middy 4G Baggin feeder rod with a softish tip – proper gear that's focused on casting and catching bream."

Sitting on his chosen rod is a Shimano Stradic reel spooled with Middy Lo-Viz 4.2lb main line. One thing that hasn't changed a great deal, though, is Russ' rig, which consists of a medium cage feeder that runs freely down to a hook link of around 12 inches and which holds a size 18 Kamasan B611 hook, perfect for his double red maggot hook bait.

"My groundbait mix is Sonubait's F1 Dark Sweet Fishmeal mixed to a stiff but fluffy consistency," explains Russ. "The reason for this, and the use of a cage feeder, is that I want the feed to explode as it hits the surface of the water, creating a attractive cloud as it sinks.

"I also include a sprinkling of fluoro pinkies and red maggots in there as free offerings to get the fish moving around.

"The key reason for my choice of groundbait, though, is the colour. There are a lot of predators in this lake, so a dark mix allows

Russ employs a basic running set-up for his feeder fishing. A cage feeder is used to release bait as it falls through the water to create a cloud and get the fish moving around and feeding hard.

the fish to move over the bait without drawing attention to themselves, whereas on a lighter mix they would be silhouetted against it. It's something that seems to really work here."

For this session Russ has chosen to fish Peg 38 along the Long Bank, as he knows from his six years as the fishery's onsite tackle-shop manager that at this time of year the bream shoal up not far off the point of the island at about six rod-lengths' range. And Russ didn't have to wait too long to find them.

After building up the swim with multiple casts of a loaded feeder, Russ' first indication sees the tip make a steady move round before a 3lb bream is hooked and netted.

With the water so cold bites today are at a premium but, as Russ points out, get the tactics right and the Old Lake can deliver weights that many would be pleased with at any time of the year.

He settles into a rhythm, recasting every five minutes or so to keep the bream fed and active – but they're not the only ones feeding. A vicious pull of the tip sees the next bite result in a very grumpy tench, one of two that make an appearance on the day.

For five hours' work on the feeder Russ is rewarded with 18 bream and two tench, with an estimated total weight of 60lb.

"It's been a brilliant session and a testimony to the quality of fishing on offer on the Old Lake at Bury Hill if you approach it right," says Russ as his slips back his catch.

"Many years ago I wouldn't have dreamt of catching bream in the winter months, in fact 60lb in the summer months was unheard of in matches back then.

"This is one of the waters that have really helped shaped my angling career. Every angler has them and they're places we will never forget, and I'd advise everyone to go back to them at least once – you might be surprised at what you find there."∎

"For five hours' work on the feeder Russ is rewarded with an estimated bag of around 60lb."

Follow Russ' tips and you could be looking at a Bury Hill bag like this!

Venues
**Linear Fisheries,
Oxfordshire**
Offering a number of large,
natural waters, Linear gives
the angler a great chance
to catch large carp in great
surroundings.

**Wyreside Lakes,
Lancashire**
A family run fishery offering
several lakes and some
superb specimen carp
fishing with fish to over 40lb.

Airfield Lakes, Norfolk
A relatively new venue run
by Nash angler Richard
Wilby, Airfield consists of
two lakes offering day-ticket
carping of superb quality
and fish to just shy of 50lb.

Specimen
Carp

Cyprinus carpio

The Facts
Record: 67lb 8oz
Max weight: 60lb+ (UK); 100lb plus (mainland Europe)
Max length: 40 inches
Specimen weight: 20lb
Spawn: June time when water reaches and remains at a specific temperature

More than any other fish swimming in our waterways, the specimen carp has the power to besot, hypnotise and drive anglers to extremes in their pursuit.

Intriguing in their behaviour, majestic in their size, compelling in their cunning, this is a species whose following has grown into the largest branch of the sport in the UK. The angling obsession with big carp has led to them being stocked more widely than almost any other species in the country.

The carp was first introduced into the UK by monks as a food source way back in the 1300s. Brought over from mainland Europe and reared in stew ponds it soon made its way into rivers and lakes, where it has thrived to this day.

Robust and willing to eat almost anything, including other fish, the carp really can pack the weight on, with UK specimens growing to in excess of 60lb – they go into triple figures in warmer waters on the Continent. For most anglers a 20lb fish is considered a notable specimen, while everyone wants at least one story of the capture of a 30-pounder to be able to recount to their friends.

Although the carp falls under one species there are actually three different types that come under the *Cyprinus carpio* banner: common, mirror and leather.

The common, as the name suggests is the most likely species you'll come across and which is defined by its complete covering in uniform small scales. The mirror is a close second and is distinguishable by its large shiny scales that follow no set format on its flanks. The leather has a completely scaleless look with smooth sides.

Found everywhere from large lakes, reservoirs and farm ponds to rivers, canals and even the smallest of streams, wherever specimen carp are present they offer the angler one of the greatest challenges in our sport.

Find 'em, feed 'em, float fish for 'em

Peg One's Lewis Baldwin proves you don't need alarms and leads to fool big carp.

Fact File
Name: Lewis Baldwin
Age: 32
Occupation: Head chef
Sponsor: Nash Peg One

Bite alarms, multiple rods and boilies are all must-have items for carp anglers all over the country, including myself. However, sometimes it pays to think outside of the box and turn to tactics that give you the edge over the norm. Float fishing for carp, on its day, can give you exactly that. Unfortunately it's become a bit of a forgotten art over recent years in favour of the next must-have gadget, but one ignored at your peril, as I found out.

For this feature I hit the banks of one of my local waters. Run by Royal Leamington Spa AA, Jubilee Pools just outside of Coventry is a lovely venue offering a pair of natural waters. I opted the smaller of the two lakes – Horseshoe – which has a good head of quality carp that love to patrol the crystal-clear margins early morning and into the evening.

My approach for this style of fishing is as simple as possible. Find the fish, get them feeding confidently then introduce a straightforward, strong rig that I know is reliable.

The Approach

It's important to actually locate the fish and observe their movements before you do anything else with this style of fishing. I've found when margin fishing for carp in clear water that the fish have preferred spots they like to feed on or near, and other areas, which appear identical to us, are often completely avoided by them. Carrying a small bucket of bait I will do a circuit of the venue until I see the fish and have the chance of watching them; then and only then will I introduce some bait. I note their patrol routes and bait two areas along this so that I've got a backup option should they get spooked off one.

Hemp, Pellets And Corn

1 Lewis' carp feed is mixed in stages. First in goes the hemp for oily attraction.

2 Next is a dose of 6mm Nash Bait Sticky Pellets for a more substantial reward.

3 Another layer of 3mm Sticky Pellets will help get them grubbing around.

4 A glug of Top Rod Sweetcorn 'N' Hemp liquid will release potent flavours.

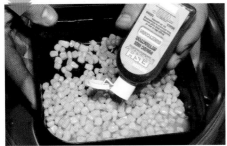

5 The hook bait also gets a shot of Fish Frenzy Sweetcorn Magic Mix.

Floats and shot
– it's as simple
as that when
stalking big
carp close in.

My bait of choice on this particular session was good old hemp, 3mm Nash Baits Fish Frenzy Sticky Pellets, 6mm Fish Frenzy Strawberry Pellets and a smattering of my hook-bait choice – sweetcorn. This was all given a liberal dose of Top Rod Hemp 'n' Corn Arouser before being introduced into my chosen swims. I keep the baited area nice and tight so as to create some competition between feeding fish and make them less wary of a hook bait being introduced.

I've already mentioned that my hook bait is sweetcorn; it's a bait that's hard to beat for carp. Even when it's not being used a great deal on a water anglers will still tip their boilies with a piece of fake corn, which goes to show how effective this little kernel is. Being bright yellow it's fantastically visual in clear water and, combined with the hemp and pellets, creates

> ## At over 22lb this fish is a great example of how effective these tactics are.

an irresistible banquet the carp will find hard to ignore.

Corn straight from the tin is a phenomenal bait but I do like to boost my hook bait a little to help it stand out, and this is where the Nash Baits Sweetcorn Frenzy Magic Mix comes in. It's a thick, gooey, sticky sweetcorn additive that when applied to your bait completely coats it and gives it a real edge, and this little trick can often pay off in spectacular fashion.

Rigging Up

Once you have the location of the carp sussed out and got them feeding confidently it's time for the all-important rig setup. I like to keep components down to a minimum and ensure that they are extremely strong. A Peg One Transformer rod in its shorter length is my preferred option as it is nice and short with a soft tip, while still offering plenty of power in reserve should it be required. This is coupled with a Shimano reel in 4000 size and it's a perfectly balanced combination. For main line I'm fishing with 8lb breaking strain, which carries the smallest insert waggler I can find attached with a pair of

Lewis likes to pep up his feed with Nash Bait liquid flavourings.

float rubbers. Using float rubbers might seem a bit 'old fashioned' but it gives me the option of changing the float in seconds should the need arise. It also means I have no bulk shot around the float, the reason for which I'll explain shortly.

Finishing the rig is a size 10 barbless hook and a single AAA shot two to three inches away, which is fished on the bottom. The idea behind having no shot around the float or up the line is that I don't want an anchor point for the line that could make it go taut. As I'm fishing at close quarters I don't want the carp to spook off a tight line, and fishing the float overdepth and lying it completely flat on the surface with the AAA shot near the hook just to keep the bait on the bottom means the line remains relatively limp throughout the water column. Bite indication with these tactics is a case of watching the swim and waiting for the float to slide away and the rod to pull round – and if you've done everything right then this shouldn't take too long.

End Result

The first thing I did when I arrived at Jubilee this morning was to walk the banks, heading straight for the area that gets the early morning sun and so is attractive to carp looking to bask and enjoy some warmth. It was the right thing to do. There, in a shallow margin, were several carp patrolling, including some good-sized fish.

This was the place for me, so I introduced ▶

The proof of the pudding – a stunning 20lb-plus common caught on the float.

my bait before setting about the task of tackling up. My cocktail of baits worked a treat. Within 15 minutes I had a number of carp ripping up the bottom to get at the hemp and pellets that were lodged in the gravel. Feeding this hard it was obvious that they were in a competitive mood, so I was confident I could get a hook bait in among them without any danger of spooking them off. After lowering a single grain of corn into the water I had to wait-all of two minutes before the float slid away and the swim erupted with carp exiting in every direction.

I could see in the clear water that the carp

that had fallen for my tactics was of a good size, so taking it nice and steady I let the rod do its job safe in the knowledge that all the components in my setup were well matched and strong enough to handle what this fish could throw at it. Before long a wonderfully conditioned chestnut-coloured common was slipping over the net cord, and at a healthy 22lb 4oz I think we can call that a result.

After catching that fish the swim was understandably deserted, so locating another shoal of carp I stripped the rig back to just a hook. This is the beauty of float rubbers, you can dismantle the whole rig and be freelining bait in seconds, really maximising any given opportunities. Casting out just a single piece of breadflake I soon had a stunning little mirror carp in the net to round my morning's fishing off nicely.

And there you have it, a basic but hugely effective tactic that caught me fish where other more modern approaches might well have seen a blank. Get out there and give it a go. ∎

Stalking Carp

Hunting big carp in the margins is great fun, but you'll need…

• **Short Rod**
You'll be fishing at close range, so go for a shorty of around seven, eight or nine feet.

• **Polarising Glasses**
Stalking is visual, the right eyewear will let you in on what's going on under the surface.

• **Sneaky Feet**
Heavy footfalls will see the fish spook before you get there – think angling ninja.

Another great looking Jubilee fish falls to Lewis' float approach.

Barbel
Barbus barbus

Torpedo-like in shape and energy the barbel is the powerhouse of Britain's running water. Its ability to fight with every last ounce of energy has seen the species become a passion for an ever-growing band of dedicated anglers who fall under the barbel's enigmatic spell.

Present right across the country in more than 50 rivers, the barbel is perfectly designed for fast-flowing water. Hugging the riverbed the water flows over the top of the fish, allowing it to stay low and hard on the bottom where it hoovers up any food it comes across. This sleek design also allows the species to give anglers a run for their money as they stay lower and power off.

The spread of barbel sees a variety of fishing situations on offer for the angler in pursuit of them. From huge, raging rivers such as the Trent and Severn through to intimate waterways such as stretches of the Warwickshire Avon and Lugg, the range of tactics and bait that can be employed to catch them is diverse. As is their size.

Averaging around 4lb, a barbel of 10lb or more is classed as a true specimen of the species, with a fish of over 14lb a catch to celebrate. They do go much bigger, though, with the British record standing at a mighty 21lb 1oz. However, the proliferation of otters has seen many of the UK's big barbel become food for the apex predator. Many believe that the bigger rivers could still produce fish of these proportions… they just need to be caught.

Venues

River Severn, Holt Fleet, Worcestershire
Run by Birmingham Anglers Association (just £35 for a full adult membership with a mass of waters to fish) the lock at Holt Fleet is famous for the quality of its barbel fishing, with some big fish to be caught.

River Trent, Beeston, Nottinghamshire
The Nottingham Anglers Association-run stretch of the Trent at Beeston offers some great, fast-river barbel fishing along a quarter of a mile bank of the waterway.

River Wye, Red Lion stretch, Bredwardine, Herefordshire
The Red Lion Hotel offers four miles of prime Wye barbel fishing along a stretch of the river known as the Moccas Fishery.

The Facts

Record: 21lb 1oz caught from the famous Adam's Mill stretch of the River Ouse, Bedford, in 2006
Max weight: 25lb
Max length: 100cm
Max age: 25 years
Specimen weight: 10lb
Spawn: July time

The long and the long of it!

A super-long hooklength was the key for four-time world champion Bob Nudd as he took on the barbel of the River Severn.

Fact File
Name: Bob Nudd
Hometown: March, Cambridgeshire
Sponsor: Browning, Van den Eynde

After a prolonged period of wet weather, Bob Nudd could be forgiven for believing his trip to the Severn would end in the disappointment of a flooded river.

So he was delighted when news reached him that the river, six feet up only five days previously, had fined down enough to make the long trip from Cambridgeshire to Bewdley worth a try.

While by no means perfect, the river was carrying 'only' 18 inches of extra water but, importantly, it was no longer rising. In fact, the colour was slowly starting to drop out. Not your typical summer Severn conditions, admittedly, but just about ideal for barbel.

Being so busy with coaching days and commitments to his sponsor, Browning, Bob Nudd doesn't have much time for pleasure fishing. A few hours here and there on the drains and commercials near to where he lives, but nothing like the River Severn at Bewdley, a fast-flowing stretch full of uncertainty. Gravel runs, shallows, huge rocks, deep pools... Bewdley has it all.

No surprise, then, that Bob's first port of call was the local tackle shop. Not only do the lads at Bewdley Tackle & Leisure have a wealth of up-to the-minute information about

the state of the river and the 'hot' swims, they also sell the pellets that Severn barbel possibly love more than any other.

Called Ambush pellets from Severn Valley Barbel Products, the pellets are hard, dark and incredibly pungent. They won't break down quickly, have a high oil content, and come in a variety of sizes from 3mm and 4mm for feeding, to 6mm, 8mm, 10mm and 12mm for hook baits. The larger sizes are even pre-drilled with a hole to allow for easy hair rigging.

Local Knowledge
Armed with plenty of Ambush pellets from the shop, Bob's next job was to find out where to fish. It was suggested that he drive out to ▶

Tackle Tips

1 Bob used the 4oz carbon tip with his Hybrid Barbel rod.

2 No place for fine tackle here!

Bob's super-long hooklength does it again as the biggest barbel of the session comes to the net.

Bob's Tackle

Rod: Browning Hybrid Barbel
Reel: Browning Black Magic FD Feeder 650
Main line: 11lb (0.22mm) Browning Hybrid Power Mono
Hooklength: 8lb (0.20mm) Browning Cenex
Hook: Size 12 Drennan Super Spade

Attaching The Pellet

Bob used the lasso technique to attach his hard pellets to the hook. The beauty of this method is that it's easy to use different sizes of pellets on the same hair, simply by changing the size of the loop.

Although Bob's hook baits were drilled with a hole through the middle so they could be hair rigged conventionally or with a Quickstop, he preferred to lasso them.

Here's how he did it:

Step 1 Tie a grinner knot in the end of the hair.

Step 2 Place your pellet inside the loop.

Step 3 Tighten the loop around the pellet and trim the tag.

Step 4 Make sure the pellet hangs neatly below the hook.

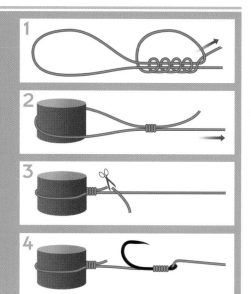

the Hawksbatch stretch of the river above the Worcestershire town, where a walk of a few hundred yards would take him into prime barbel country.

These swims, he was told, wouldn't necessarily produce the biggest barbel in the area, but they were more reliable than most, especially on a river that had been up and down more often than a fiddler's elbow since the season's start.

It's worth pointing out that Bob Nudd was given no special

Once the barbel had a taste for his pellets, bites started to come more frequently.

treatment when it came to his day on the river. Anyone can fish here for the price of a £6 day permit from the patrolling bailiff.

Every swim is numbered, but some are more comfortable to fish than others. There are several platforms that have been positioned in the water, but obviously at some times these are too far away from the water, while at others, they'll be covered. Forget your easy-access commercials, Bewdley is a real river!

Bob selected a swim that looked perfect for his feeder approach. Flowing quite hard, it was about 40 yards wide but the key for Bob was a steadier glide running between 15 and 20 yards from his fishing position. To Bob, this looked like the river was running over a gravel bed and he was sure it would hold some barbel.

Feeder Is King

With the river flowing far too fast for anything other than a feeder approach, Bob was soon setting

Conditions might look more like winter than summer, but the barbel didn't seem to mind.

up his powerful 12ft feeder rod. The rod comes with three tips and Bob selected the middle one, which was marked '4oz carbon'. He wanted a tip that would bend enough in the flow to allow him to see drop-back bites easily and he felt the 4oz would be perfect. The 6oz tip would be called into play only on a flooded river, while the 2oz would be employed in slow flows and low-water conditions.

As for the feeder itself, a medium-sized

Lasso Rig
The lasso is a great way of hair rigging when you might be using different sizes of bait.

blockend fitted the bill, but Bob made sure he bought some extra-heavy weights from the shop before fishing. Using long-nosed pliers, he removed the weight from the side of the feeder and replaced it with an angled lead weight weighing 2oz. This was very much a 'suck-it-and-see' exercise. He knew that he wouldn't need a lighter weight than this… but he might need a heavier one.

With a tough 11lb main line and 8lb hooklength, Bob felt his gear was 'man' enough for the conditions, and for the fish he hoped to catch.

The Session
With everything ready Bob explained how he intended to start by making frequent casts to get some feed into the swim. This feed was a mix of 3mm and 4mm pellets. He didn't expect a bite for at least an hour, by which time hopefully the barbel would have found the feed and would then home in on his 8mm pellet hook bait.

First problem he encountered was casting. With the abundance of bankside vegetation and trees above, an overhead cast was impossible, and the 5ft hooklength also made an underarm swing very difficult. In the end, he managed a sort of 45-degree lob and after a few trial efforts he was depositing the feeder perfectly, slightly upstream of his fishing position and about 20 yards out in the river.

Bob then had to decide how to pack the pellets in the feeder. This might sound like an

Here's How To Make Bob's Simple Rig...
Step 1 Thread a link swivel up the main line and slide it right up out of the way.
Step 2 Thread a normal swivel onto the main line, pulling around 20 inches of line through the swivel.
Step 3 Tie a twisted 6in loop in the end of the line, incorporating the swivel into the bottom of the loop.
Step 4 Tie a 9in loop above the twisted loop, ensuring the link swivel runs inside this new loop. Add the feeder to the link swivel.
Step 5 Finally, attach a 5ft hooklength to the swivel at the bottom of the twisted loop.

Feeder Tips

1 Filling the feeder up to the top of the cylinder ensured perfect release.

2 Two ounces of lead were needed on the feeder.

3 Enlarge the holes in the base (left) to release its contents faster.

easy one, but if the pellets were too tightly packed, none came out. If they were too loose in the feeder, the smaller 3mms fell out during the cast. He was soon filling the feeder to the top of the cylinder with pellets, so that there was a little 'air' in the top once he closed the cap. Perfect!

Finally, rod position. Once the feeder had landed on the bottom, Bob released some line from his reel until the feeder held bottom and the tip had a healthy bend. He didn't need to keep the rod tip right up in the air to keep as much line as possible out of the water, as he would have done if he was fishing further out.

Half an hour into the session, and after making a dozen or so casts, Bob saw a slight tap on his tip. Just as he was considering whether a small fish had pecked at the pellet, the tip banged round and he instinctively lifted the rod.

The smile on his face said it all, as a barbel powered off towards the middle. It was no match for Bob's tackle, though, and a River Severn four-pounder soon lay in his landing net. Over the next two hours, four more barbel fell, with the biggest fish close to 7lb. All came to 8mm pellet and the best was saved until last, with the rod almost being dragged from his hands seconds after casting.

It had been a great session and testimony to the right combination of brilliant bait, the correct tackle, superb local knowledge... oh, and a four-time world champion's deadly skills! ∎

Five cracking barbel. All swam off strongly after a short time in Bob's huge keepnet.

Top Pellets
Severn Valley Barbel Products pellets. Hard, pungent and perfect!

ADE KIDDELL'S
RIVER FEEDER ESSENTIALS

Spicy Sausage Halibut Pellets

Spicy Sausage Halibut Pellets are perfect for packing into an open end feeder. Pack them in as hard as you can, for maximum attraction and minimum feed.

Hemp and Spicy Sausage Liquid

Pour a generous helping of the Hemp and Spicy Sausage Liquid over your Halibut Pellets to increase the pulling power when in the river.

Pellet O's

Save time when you get to the river bank by grabbing a tub of Pellet O's; these Pre-drilled pellets will save you valuable time when preparing your hookbaits ready for the hair.

Ade Kiddell
Specimen Angler

Spicy Sausage Halibut Pellets available in:
• 4mm • 6mm • 8mm

Pellet O's also available in:
• 8mm Krill • 12mm Krill • 8mm Crab
• 12mm Crab • 8mm Spicy Sausage
• 12mm Spicy Sausage • 8mm Halibut
• 12mm Halibut

INGENIOUS. IRRESISTIBLE

sonubaits.com

Perch

Perca fluviatilis

An iconic British species, the perch is the spike-laden bullyboy of our freshwaters, bristling with attitude and armour in equal measure.

Nurturing a greedy desire to beat other fish to any bait in the water from an early age, the perch is often one of the first species the novice fisherman is likely to catch, and to need to use a disgorger to unhook for that very reason. In ounce sizes they roam in shoals and are found on pretty much every water type around, making them a favourite with pleasure and match anglers alike – but it's when they grow over the pound mark that the fun really begins.

Perca fluviatilis is an out-and-out predator, its striped camouflage and stocky build making it a short-range ambush master. Lacking the slice-and-dice dentistry of the pike and zander, however, the perch instead will knock and strike its prey to stun and disable them before engulfing the unlucky baitfish within its cavernous mouth, from which there's no escape.

Over the past decade the size of big perch has grown, thanks mainly to the bait-filled havens of commercial fisheries where the specimen perch can gorge on prey as an apex predator. Having sprung back from the dark days of the 1960s and 1970s where ulcer-based disease decimated UK populations, a perch of 4lb was a bona fide giant, before the first-ever 5lb-plus specimen was banked in 1985 to set a new British record. It took more than 20 years to break this barrier, but from 2006 onwards no fewer than three new record fish have been recorded, with two of those having been over 6lb.

Venues

Tring Reservoir, Hertfordshire
This large water has produced both the British record and the largest brace of perch ever caught in the UK.

Stream Valley, Sussex
A day-ticket commercial carp water that's produced two of the last three British records.

River Ouse, Milton Keynes
Plenty of big perch getting fat on crayfish have made the Ouse a hot ticket for specimens.

The Facts

Record: 6lb 3oz caught from Tring Reservoir, Hertfordshire, by Ken Brown in 2011
Max weight: 7lb
Max length: 20 inches
Max age: 20 years
Specimen weight: 3lb
Spawn: As early as March conditions depending

Hunting Canal Perch

Over the winter and early spring Dan has made the Grand Union canal his second home, covering miles and miles of towpath in search of perch on lures. In that time he's banked what must be hundreds of fish including two over 4lb – one hell of a fish from a canal – learning their routines and feeding habits. Here he gives up the secrets to his hard-earned success – get out there and have a go yourself.

Canal Perching

Hit the lures, keep it simple and put in the legwork and you could soon be latching into stripey stunners like this, as Fox's Dan Sales explains.

Fact File
Name: Dan Sales
Age: 28
Occupation: Builder
PB canal perch: 4lb 4oz

Back in winter the rivers were high and running chocolate brown and I was just about on the verge of going insane. I've always preferred the roaming approach, finding the fish by testing different pieces of water for a relatively short amount of time, seeing what they're up to and tapping into their funny feeding habits at this cold time of the year. But, with the river situation as it was I decided to turn my hand to a bit of stillwater fishing. The trouble with this was that the lakes were mostly frozen or devoid of life, leaving me just one option – the local canal system, and specifically the Grand Union.

With plenty of boat traffic, flowing inlets, cover and movement in general it had the potential to produce fish whatever the weather. Not being a massive fan of sitting behind a pod, waiting for a bite and generally freezing my arse off, the only species I could see worth targeting without being static were perch. After a bit of research on the internet I found that most parts of the GUC could produce a specimen stripey, with reports

showing that the north, middle and southern stretches were all capable of fish to over 4lb.

Not knowing much about where I was going it seemed right to adopt a walking and casting approach, not spending too much time in any one area unless it produced fish. For this work lures are the obvious choice. The excitement when a fish slams into a piece of rubber or plastic is second to none. I've had some great success on the rivers with small rubber jigs mounted directly onto a small jigheads.

Because the canals have very little flow at all, if any, I could really fine my kit down in hope of nailing every fish in the swim. On the sharp end a 3.5g jighead with a size 1 hook holding a small, 3in rubber lure fits perfectly in those big old gobs, but as much as I like to catch specimen-sized fish, my canal sessions were more about locating fish first then trying to single out the bigger ones.

Tackle Up

With perch being relatively small in size you can fish very light for them, making even the smallest of fish great fun to catch. Short spinning rods of anything between 5ft 11in ▸

On The Menu

Keeping up with what the perch want means having a varied selection of lures. Dan won't leave home without covering the basics including:

1 Large worms – Sometimes the perch just want a big meal and you can put plenty of action into one of these.

2 Grubs – Part worm, part fish, the curly tail on these things can drive the fish mad.

3 Pin tails – They don't provide masses of movement but on the right day the deft lift of a pin tail is all the fish want.

4 Jointed minnow – Loads of action and as close to a small baitfish as you can get. A must-have in your lure bag.

5 Drop-shot shad – These are designed to provide maximum movement as they are lifted and dropped.

6 Flashy – With canal clarity changing from lock to lock adding a flash of colour is a must.

and 7ft are perfect for the short chucks a canal requires. A casting weight between 1g and 15g is spot-on, but the lighter the better. Small reels loaded with 6lb mono or light braid are sufficient; perch make very short, jagged runs so there's no need for heavy line and this combination of tackle will see you getting the best sport from every fish you hook.

I must have walked well over 40 miles of towpath trying to locate fish. Because of this I need my kit to be small and ultra-light. My entire tackle list consists of a small case loaded with technicolour rubber lures of all shapes and sizes, a couple of packs of jigheads, forceps, a couple of spools of line and a camera all stuffed into a small backpack. Attached to the backpack is a roll-up landing mat and a small trout net. Rod in hand and away you go! I can't think of any other style of coarse fishing that is so accessible and mobile.

Think Predator

As with any predator fishing you should always try to think like they do. Where would you hide if you were sneaking up on prey? Canals are full of features, with my favourite being boats. Look for those permanently

Features on canals are key. The far wall, for instance, can be a patrolling and holding spot for perch. Cast as close as you can and let the lure fall to the bottom before making your retrieve.

Sometimes it's the features that you can't see that hold the fish. The bottom of the slopes down to the centre channel can often be havens for baitfish, and the perch will not be far away.

moored or, even better, ones that have been neglected and left to the elements. Weed will start to grow on the hull, which attracts baitfish, and in turn the perch won't be too far away.

Any cover is worth a chuck, be it a bridge creating shade, a wall making the perfect ambush point, a drop-off, a tree… anything that looks like it could hide a fish is always worth a few casts. Very rarely do I catch anything in water that doesn't look like it will produce. Try to tap into their world!

When casting and retrieving I always try to get as close to my chosen feature as possible, let the jig sink completely to the bottom and start my retrieve. All too often I see guys fishing at a fast pace and not really putting enough thought into how their lure is acting under the surface. Have a little test jig in the margins and see how your lure reacts to different twitches – you want to make it look injured and really tempt the perch into striking, even if he's not really hungry!

Perch can really blow your mind with how fussy they can be. I've seen a group of fish smashing small fry, killing quite a few but not eating a single thing, almost as if they were bored with the ones that weren't moving – a real eye-opener. With that in mind I prefer to jig my lures up through the water and then back to the canal bed, creating a small puff of mud each time I jerk it closer to me. Keeping your rod tip high you can really create a movement using 'sink and draw' that's irresistible.

Some days the fish are very hungry and strikes are savage, but then come the days when the fish really don't want to play ball, which is when I'll opt for a very slow retrieve. I'm pretty positive you can annoy a fish into striking even if they aren't all that hungry. I also go fishing with friends and have found that if we fish the same spot, the constant retrieve of lures through an area can work the fish into a striking frenzy where, if you'd just made a couple of casts yourself, you might not have got anything.

Colour

Keep an eye on the water colour. One pound (a piece of water between locks) can be massively different in clarity and colour from another, meaning ▸

With just a rucksack, rod, reel and a few other basics Dan stores his kit in his van and does a couple of hours after work. Which is exactly what he did on this session.

A light rod-and-reel setup, such as in the new Fox Rage Ultron range, combined with low-diameter braid is spot-on for perch.

With perch being very sensitive to light levels, the shade of a bridge can be a productive spot to try.

that the colour of the lure you use can play a huge part in getting a take.

I've found that with clearer water a dark lure will work and with murky water a vivid, bright lure will produce the goods. It's really down to changing things about as much as possible until you find the perfect pattern, and another case for trying it in the margin before you go for gold.

This style of 'smash and grab' fishing really suits me down to the ground. Having to work five to six days a week means my fishing time is really limited, but with just a rod and backpack chucked in the back of the van I can grab a few hours, normally still in my work gear, and bag some cracking fish. The best part of the day is usually dusk, so I arrive just as the fish start to prowl. Over the last few months, after putting in the initial legwork to find the hotspots, I've caught loads of perch with a

good average size, topped by a fish of 4lb 4oz by using this approach.

It's not complicated and I think so many more people would enjoy this style of fishing if they gave it a go. The main things to remember are to keep it simple, think about your technique and swap things about until you find something that works.

One word of advice, though, is always respect others. Canals are used heavily by boaters who don't like their paintwork being chipped by jigheads or their peaceful lives disturbed by noisy anglers. Think about what you are doing, keep the peace and you'll be left to your own devices bagging perch after perch! ∎

Online Lures

Have a look around the web to buy lures perfect for bagging big canal perch.

- harrissportsmail.com
- sovereignsuperbaits.co.uk
- lure-world.com
- agmdiscountfishing.co.uk
- lure-anglers-shop.co.uk
- lureanglers.co.uk

During Dan's session on the Grand Union he caught several stunning perch getting on for 3lb. Dusk proved to be the best time, as Dan predicted, but it was staying on the move and keeping the lures changing and moving that produced the results.

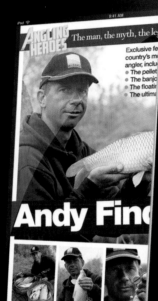

Striped Specimens

There's never been a better time to break your perch PB, and Gardner Tackle's Alan Stagg is the man to help you do it.

Fact File
Name: Alan Stagg
Age: 29
Occupation: Media manager Gardner Tackle
Perch PB: 5lb 4oz

Is there any more impressive sight than a big perch on the bank - stripey, prehistoric, bristling with the anger of a hunter that's just become the hunted.

The fact that pretty much every angler in the country has caught one in miniature only adds to the awe that these specimen fish command. When you're used to seeing them at an average of 5oz anything over 2lb is monstrous, over 3lb almost breathtaking.

And there's never been a better time to get out there and target them either. The rise of the commercial carp water has produced the well documented side-effect of growing fish to record breaking proportions. Raised on a glut of bait and shoals of fat silver fish, specimen 'sergeants' have never had it so good, and neither have anglers looking to catch them.

But there's still the question of unlocking the stripey potential of your local water when it comes to rigs, tackle and bait. Gardner Tackle's Alan Stagg seems to have the answers though, having landed a number of impressively big fish from many different venues. Today we catch up with him at the famous Stream Valley Lakes in Sussex, where he reveals his tactics to help you land a new personal-best stripey.

Turn To The Prawn

At the heart of Alan's winning approach is a bait that's grown massively in popularity and success with commercial perch over recent years, the prawn.

Such is the appeal of the pink crustacean it's a bait that's become synonymous with modern perch fishing. Having proved the downfall of a number of specimens, including the previous record, its track record speaks for itself, making it the bait of choice for our expert Alan Stagg when targeting commercial waters.

"I was pretty sceptical about fishing with prawns to start off with," said Alan, "but it catches a good proportion of fish at Stream Valley and as it get used more and more at other fisheries its also proving a great big-perch catcher across the UK."

Alan opts for a traditional specimen approach when fishing prawn, three rods on alarms, each with a leger setup – and the watchwords of 'minimum resistance' at the forefront of his mind.

"The aim is for the perch to feel nothing when they take the bait. If there's resistance they'll eject it, so you have to make it as easy for them as possible to move the prawn while still registering a bite," he adds.

His rig for the job is simplicity itself. A Gardner 1oz pear lead on a running leger sits up against a Covert buffer bead. This covers a size 8 swivel which holds a Gardner Q ring, allowing Alan to quickly change his 14in, 5lb Target fluorocarbon hooklength if necessary. The large diameter on the lead's swivel means the 6lb Hydroflo main line runs through it effortlessly, not giving the fish a hint that their snack comes loaded with a size 8 Wide Gape Gardner Talon Tip hook.

> **A big perch for the cameras was a tall order, but he's done it with this stunning fish.**

For hook bait Alan opts for a large prawn a couple of inches long, mounted through the centre.

"I've not found any need for hair rigging. The perch tend to just inhale the whole bait and hooking the prawn through the middle gives a good hold," explains Alan.

Fishing three swims - two under overhanging branches and another two rod lengths straight out from the bank – Alan baits up with a meaty concoction designed to attract and hold the perch. This comprises a number of chopped-up prawns and dendrabaena worms along with red maggots, which is 'Spombed' out at the start of the session and after every fish or bite.

"I'll put around three-quarters of a pint of the mix out at the start of the session and top it up when necessary," says Alan. "When the temperature really drops off I'll cut this back and add flavoured liquids in to keep the attraction but cut down the food content."

Back on the bank Alan's bite indication comes from alarms and the use of lightweight Gardner Nano Bug bobbins set on a long drop to give the perch plenty of scope to take with confidence.

"The perch will move in twos or threes and when they're in your swim you'll often get carp-like line bites as they start feeding. Bites tend to be slow lifts of the bobbin as the perch picks up the bait and moves off. I just hope they're playing ball today."

The Session

Alan's not known as a big-fish expert for nothing, and although catching a

A basic running-leger rig will fool even the most cunning of perch.

big perch for the cameras was a tall order, a few hours into the session he's done just that.

A couple of bleeps of his alarm on the rod positioned under the overhanging branches and Alan struck into a fish of 2lb 14oz. A show of just how powerful the pull of the prawn is to big perch.

There was better to come, though. Just after dark the same rod went again, this time with a fish of 3lb 7oz coming to the waiting net. A great result. ∎

Alan's prawn attack resulted in the biggest fish of the day and the only one over the magic 3lb barrier. Backed up by a high two, it's an impressive brace.